# Jeannette Walls

## Biography

A Life Beyond The Glass Castle

Mark Whittington

# Table of Contents

Chapter 1: **A Prologue of False Starts**

Chapter 2: **TRAPPED**

Chapter 3: **TREASURES**

Chapter 4: **WILD AND HOME**

Chapter 5: **Acknowledgements**

# Chapter 1

# A Prologue of False Starts

When I collapsed, I needed to know what to do straight away. It was a chronic problem, but it remained a crisis. I was unwell, alone, and incapacitated. And I wondered, 'What should I do now?', 'How can I help myself right now?' And then there was a flash of rage: 'There's a thriving self-help market out there, wonderful awareness and discourse on holistic well-being from amazing experts, but I don't know what to do right now to help this important time of my.'

I needed to know what to do for the next ten minutes, and perhaps the next. But I didn't have anything concrete to draw on. There are no concrete basis for trust.

This became increasingly illogical throughout the months.

I chose to find out.

I needed to find out.

I needed to know what to do in the following 10 minutes.

Well, I found out. I researched, studied, and chose to write about it, which is why we're here. Hello, dear reader Chum. However, I discovered far more than I had anticipated, so I had no idea how or where to begin this book.

Starting can be difficult. Especially with anything that seems significant.

For me, however, it is an epic journey. I'm writing about what I've learned and experienced in recent years. I had not expected my life to turn out or crumble the way it did. But here I am, remarkably intact.

My dear reader Chum, I made several attempts to start this book. In the spirit of honesty, here are the various ways and my feelings on them:

It's been quite a journey... Oh my, not a good start. Begin anew...

Roses are red, violets are blue. I'm going to make a cup of tea and perhaps take a poo.

Bring yourself together, Hart. It's time to get serious.

Where is the life manual? I hadn't felt good since my late teens. I had frequent infections and injuries. Bronchitis, tonsillitis, pericarditis, costochondritis, gastroenteritis, labyrinthitis, too many 'itises' to mention, followed by a blood clot, slipped disc, ankle and knee ligament rips, adrenal fatigue, chronic migraines, parasites, cysts, and blah blah blah blah BLAH. There wasn't a few months, or even weeks, that went by without another 'illness' rearing its ugly head. Finally, every morning I awoke with dread about how I was going to find the energy to get through the day. And I had no idea why this was all happening. Neither did the physicians, who I was frequently handed between. It started to scare me. I felt as if I lacked the crucial answers to all of the amazing knowledge on mind and body that is available today. I simply felt overwhelmed. It seems that I needed to read one book on mindfulness, another on sleep patterns, another on the mind-body link, one on habits, objectives, and purpose, one on hormones, one on dopamine alone, one on trauma, one on caffeine, and one on alcohol. Are coffee and alcohol even acceptable? One person responded yes, and the other said no. Continue reading... A book on power postures, one on cold baths, one on silent retreats, one on expressing rage, and another on soya beans. It was just too much. What were the fundamentals that provided me with a foundation for change?

If you've ever heard the phrase "coming home to yourself," have you felt a sense of serenity, knowing it must be real but having no idea what it means? I looked around for a few answers.

I dug deeper and eventually came up with an amazing revelatory definition: "Coming home to yourself" is operating from a place of calm and authority, where you are free to be who you are (your true self), rather than being buffeted by others' opinions of you or worldly measures of success. Essentially, full self-acceptance. Okay, please, I want some of that. Surely it is the secret to being holistically healthy? Living as my authentic, crazy self.

For many, it would have been an unremarkable event in life. A dog walk. Wearing walking boots to navigate a muddy route through a tiny wood. But I hadn't needed slippers or walking boots in years, and I was beaming wider than usual. Such a smile was also incompatible with the slick mud underfoot; at the age of fifty, I'd suddenly developed a fear of falling down. (It happened virtually overnight; now, I never go to the restroom without my phone in case I stumble!)

Suddenly, the gravity of this otherwise commonplace situation struck me. I noticed a bunch of bluebells. Again, there is nothing of great consequence to report. Except, you see, I had been wanting to see a bluebell wood for a long time. I looked up, past the clump that had stopped me on the trail. There they were all, a gorgeous blue flowing down a steep slope into a pure river. My breath was completely taken away. I burst out crying!

The tears were shed for more than just the beauty of the bluebells. It had taken exactly nine years to build up the physical strength to see bluebells in the spring. I cried, too, in recognition of the previous decade of terrible health and how much my sickness had robbed from me throughout my life. I had 'all the feels', as the young folks say.

Wait, I seem to be starting my book at the conclusion. I may not be the greatest literary genius, but even I understand that starting a book from the beginning is often the best way to go.

I believe I am avoiding and thus trapping myself in sharing truthfully from the outset. Okay, enough false starts; I've chosen how to begin. I'll simply try to tell you my story.

We each have a story. I know I wouldn't be where I am today if individuals hadn't ventured to tell their tales, especially those of suffering and triumph. They made me feel connected, moved, heard, encouraged, and informed. I'm not sure if my narrative will do that for you, but I believe I've learned some valuable lessons along the road. That is the point for me. I want to share the solutions that were critical to my recovery - from long-term disease to living a lot more meaningful, liberated, and joyful life. I believe I am writing the book I needed. If you're still reading, I'd want to say hello. This is our third time together, and it's been a lot of fun. I hope my tale can benefit yours. However, as a great friend of mine usually says when it comes to advise, 'Take what you want, leave the rest.'

So, here we are. The true start. My Dear Reader Chum, get yourself settled. It's not a particularly happy start, but there's no need to worry. I'll be your cozy, warm comfort blanket (metaphorically, because I don't intend to knock on your door and smother my six-foot-one body all over you unexpectedly - sorry, it's gone crazy). Spoiler alert: the book ends happily. So, if you're currently dealing with personal challenges, remember that you can get through it. More than satisfactory. You already are. You are fabulous. Fact. Whether you believe it now or not.


Okay, that's enough about you. Return to me…

# Chapter 2: TRAPPED

## An Ending Was The Real Start

I realized it was pointless to call an ambulance.

I was alone and had just slumped on the floor of my living room, accompanied by worried licks from Peggy, my dog, who was attempting to help me. I couldn't move much because I was so exhausted. I recall adding, "It's extremely rare to die of exhaustion." "I'm not okay, but it's okay," I said, attempting to comfort both Peggy and myself. I felt so weak. As if I did not exist. As if I were drifting away. After three decades, I understood enough about chronic illness to predict that my vital signs would most likely register as normal, and I would be sent home with no clear answers.

Perhaps I wasn't terrified because I had nothing left to give. I was simply sad. I just laid there. And waited. My body would either start to recover or fade away. I couldn't do anything about it. I sank deeper into the rug, letting out a loud sigh. Regardless of the scenario, there was relief. When you reach the end of the path, there is nothing else to do but let go. There is no longer an option between going somewhere, working, or pushing on. You're compelled to simply be who you are in the moment. And wait. In retrospect, moments like this, which people refer to as the beginning of the end, can be joyous. They are stories to be enjoyed and explored.

I'd like to apologize right away and emphasize how tremendously fortunate I am to live in such a privilege-rich society. I am acutely aware of the tremendous inequity and suffering that exist in this world. However, I believe that rejecting our stories out of guilt will only make matters worse. Our anguish and pain are acceptable. Every story matters.

The relief of reaching the end of the path turned into an

overwhelming sense of aloneness. In that time, I didn't feel like I had anyone to contact. How could I explain my fatigue? There was no definite diagnosis (which would emerge years later).

After a few hours, thankfully, I was able to muster the energy to crawl to the lavatory, accompanied by Peggy. I burst into uncontrolled sobs, partially out of relief that I'd been able to move, but also because I was confronted with how I truly felt. I told myself that all I could do was sleep and recuperate for a few days and then go from there.

After four days, I still felt like a ghost. Hollow. Nonetheless, I was so used to finding methods to stay calm and go on - or at least simply carry on - that I summoned my remaining power to remain with my companions as scheduled. Particularly because it was Christmas and I didn't want to feel any more alone. I am a little scared. Can I just be in a ball? They smiled sweetly and added, 'You're here with complete acceptance and love, whoever you are.' A fantastic script.

Everything I felt within erupted furiously that Christmas, in stark contrast to the twinkling lights and merry music. I just tried to keep going and find some lightness. Looking back, it's clear that I felt compelled to persevere. So much of my life has been like this. Nobody had any answers for me. I became enraged that my body was betraying my passion for life. I was filled with dreams and ambitions, yet my body felt under attack. The frequent infections and viruses had severely debilitated me; simply throwing antibiotics and anti-inflammatories at them (all antis for the itises) was no longer sustainable as the years passed. I was continually having to say no to things I really wanted to do because I couldn't do them freely, completely, or cheerfully.

I was fighting a war and not winning.

I've made a decision. This fall, this conclusion, might only be the beginning. The beginning of getting some answers, of regaining my health so that I might have space and energy for excitement, possibilities, and a pain-free future. I laid in bed, my beloved dog's soft fur next to my arm, the distant hum of my friends' sing-along, which I so desperately wanted to join, echoing some joy into my room, and I chose to believe that this could be my catalyst.

This would be my official start.

# The Sliding Cat

It was dusk when I first encountered the collapsing moment at home. I was sleeping on my front, head facing the garden, when I noticed the sky disappearing. I decided to push my body onto my back so that I could watch the particularly magnificent English winter sky become completely dark through the skylights above me. It seemed like quite the accomplishment, not just the physical exertion, but also the thought of confronting my situation full on rather than burrowing - literally and symbolically - into my sitting room carpet.

I received a wonderful gift in doing so.

As I turned over, my neighbour's enormous tabby cat hopped onto the bricks at the base of the skylight windows. It decided to go up to the roof, which I believe it has done previously, but not on such a chilly day with some frozen pockets on the glass. This bulbous cat climbed three-quarters of the way up the snowy skylights with much hilarious pedalling, but the surface was too slippery. It was trying to keep its dignity but couldn't get a sale! The adorable cat had to accept that it would not win this beautiful war. Our gazes met. Despite my predicament, I smiled (if I'd had the stamina, I would have laughed even harder), and the cat appeared humiliated and outraged in equal measure. Making it even hilarious.

This little moment, in which I managed to grin despite everything, taught me that there can be treasures in the dark. My Dearest Reader Chum, I truly believe that joy may exist even in our darkest moments.

My mind was stirred. If I discovered this treasure on one of my most difficult days, can I dare to believe there could be more? Is it possible that there is armor and answers within darkness?

# Darkness

I had been trained to believe that gloomy situations should be fought, corrected, and feared. My reaction was the same whether the gloom was caused by illness, sadness, a challenging job scenario, an argument, or simply a light hour of worry over something commonplace. 'This is not on,' a voice within would say in my most severe, posh, army-colonel-slash-boarding-school-matron voice - enjoy that image. Aren't we always supposed to be pleasant, positive, and uncomplaining? That was my script, and it is for many of us. But as we continue this adventure together, My Dear Reader Chum (or MDRC, if I may … because I already feel we are friends), I will show you how much rubbish I now think this to be.

While I now understand that joy is always present, I also acknowledge that darkness is a part of existence. Darkness is permitted. We are entitled to feel, and we will naturally experience sadness, disappointment, anxiety, wrath, shame, and everything from hysterical laughter to panic on the same day. When we allow ourselves to feel these emotions, our fear of them and our tough situations decreases.

I understand that this is simple to say, especially in retrospect. We still need to go through it.

The end, my rock bottom, may have been the beginning, but it would take a few more years of struggle - of darkness - to get to the other side.

## The Cave

I'll never forget a vivid sight that came to me a few weeks after collapsing. I was bleary-eyed, so I'm afraid this may just make sense to me, but I'm plunging in. Stay with me in case you appreciate the metaphor that follows.

After staring at the rock for a long time, thinking of it simply as my nemesis, a devastating impediment to my route in life, I began to approach it with a little more curiosity. I realized it was engraved in the shape of a door. I slowly pulled the door open, ready to enter whatever was inside. It was dark. Musty. Dank. A cavern. With slimy and muddy walls. I proceeded over the cold, stone floor until another entrance at the other end of the cave become dimly visible. Somehow, I knew the door was one that I would be able to enter at the appropriate time. And I would feel renewed. The power and knowledge required for the journey out would continue with me, allowing me to live the rest of my life to the fullest. I know, MDRC (My Dear Reader Chum, in case you forgot - RUDE). It's a lot. All I can say is that it seemed practical. And sensible.

What if I decided to quit fighting my body? Certainly, after years of attempting to avoid and cure, I had no fight left in me. What if the only way out was to confront the mystery of my feelings full on? To navigate the dark, muddy, and murky cave until I reached the door on the other side.

# Hidden

I've had the extremely humbling pleasure of hearing from thousands of people that the character I played in my sitcom, Miranda, helped them accept who they are. I was writing a character that was striving to fit in, but lacked the confidence to express herself fully. I had no clue it would resonate on such a large scale.

Many folks would tell me about their socially awkward 'Miranda moments'. I am pleased to inform that I have recently had my own. Miranda's Miranda Moment! I was in a doctor's office, and when my name was called, I didn't know my purse strap was wrapped around the arm of the chair I was sitting in. I approached the doctor with the chair shrieking behind me, as if I had brought it as a pet.

I remember being moved to tears when a young adolescent girl wrote to me and said she hadn't been coming to school in a while due to bullying because she was exceptionally lanky and tall. In reality, she stated that with her newfound confidence in herself, the comments gradually disappeared. I was extremely moved. Others - many, in fact - informed me that learning to embrace themselves was the catalyst for healing in many other areas of their lives.

Then I focused on a less comical way of thinking about it. I read in palliative care worker Bronnie Ware's book, The Top Five Regrets of the Dying, that the top regret was, 'Wishing I had the guts to live life according to myself, not the life others expected of me.' That crushed my heart, MDRC.

We are shaped by our family, our connections, the places we live, the groups we belong to, and the stories we tell ourselves or have been told. However, these things might lead us to hide our wonderful, unique genuine identities.

# Fame

Before I continue with my story, I'd like to make a little aside. I know we've only just begun, so please be patient. This aside is about the f-word. And I believe it is more of a curse than the commonly used f-word. As I like to say, nothing beats a good 'fuck' from time to time. Sorry!

But celebrity is quite the beast. I remember being photographed at Wimbledon and a paparazzi asking me, rather aggressively, to remove my sunglasses, which I refused. He mocked me: 'Ha ha, certainly a big night last night!' It wasn't spoken in a cheerful tone, but rather with the snarky assumption that I was masking bloodshot swollen eyes produced by excessive alcohol intake. When I spend 99 percent of my time watching TV, bathing, or snacking, I frequently do so simultaneously. In this case, I didn't remove my sunglasses because I was experiencing symptoms related to light sensitivity. Plus, I'd done my eye makeup horribly, and I was afraid I'd come across as a bad Alice Cooper impersonator.

There were definitely aspects of my employment that contributed to weariness (celebrity is a trap in itself). But disease would have occurred anyway.

While we're here, I'd want to state unequivocally that I do not recommend fame. It is an unusual monster. Even if you aspire to something, which I pronounce to be foolish, you have no control over whether or not it happens. It is imposed upon you. It happens when you have a moment of fame (or notoriety). That popularity is not your fault! You're just doing your job, and it's unavoidable that people will like you, which leads to fame. And suddenly it just takes. Fame is not a friend; it is a taker. The system that wanted to make you famous also wants to bring you down, seemingly with joy.

I didn't object to any fame or criticism. I loved the ride while keeping my expectations in check. In some respects, I think it's a good thing I became famous.

People must realize that celebrity does not bring joy. It is not the gift of a sliding cat. I believe there is just one positive aspect to celebrity. And that one thing is improved customer service. (But even that stings since it's annoying that not everyone receives good customer service.)

Let me tell you something: when you see a happy famous person, it's not because they're famous. Unless they've recently had excellent customer service.

So, no, this comedic actress' weariness was not caused by her rock-and-roll lifestyle. I refer the honorable reader to the previously described 'night out', which consisted of wallowing in a bath with food.

# The Elephant

Speaking of wallowing, if I had to pick my favorite animal, it would be the emotionally astute and magnificent elephant. One of my fondest recollections is scrubbing one with a broom in a muddy river while it wallowed and rolled while visiting a refuge in Thailand. However, my elephant story becomes less cheerful here. To say the least. Buckle up.

Reflecting on the idea of our inner selves being hidden, I feel I now understand why I responded so fiercely - viscerally - to a movie at the sanctuary about how the elephants they rescue are captured. Wild elephants are captured and placed in small wooden cages.

After days of this, an elephant realizes there's no hope. It realizes that if it stays quiet and still, it will not be damaged. It has been beaten to submission. This elephant must forget about its younger, wilder self.

As the humans remove the wooden cage, they bind the elephant's feet with chains. If it runs, it will fall. It can only lumber at a slow enough pace to avoid a damaging impact to the ground. Eventually, it becomes a slave to its human master. A wild animal working in the tourism sector.

It's a sad and dramatic image. We're horrified, not only because of the horrific, appalling animal abuse, but also because I believe there may be some parallels with our own life. Many people have experienced, to varied degrees, abuse, being told to shut up, being pushed to make decisions against their will, and having their rights violated. We may have all, to some extent, been pushed and shoved by individuals and institutions that are not in our best interests, no matter how superficially innocent and possibly inadvertently.

And this is what I meant previously when I mentioned 'so-called right worldly methods'.

Worldly 'rules' that shout things like be kind and polite at all costs, because being nice and polite is what gets you where; Get good grades even if you aren't intellectual; don't display any embarrassing feelings; be outgoing, humorous, and intriguing because that's the only way to 'succeed' socially. Know exactly what you want to do, have a professional path planned out, and put a lot of pressure on yourself to have a job that makes you look and sound successful; Be small, sweet, and feminine if you're a woman, and for goodness sake, don't be too loud, opinionated, or angry, yet take up your space and seize success; Try not to wrinkle or age, and shift your face to stay young. Fit in to ensure you have a 'cool' circle of mates. get on the property ladder or live in a camper van or tiny house, nothing in between because you don't want to be boring; but don't be weird; don't just be a stay-at-home parent, also run a business or a charity, but look after the children perfectly so that they don't suffer from any emotional issues, keep proving you're a good person.

by satisfying everyone else's needs since it is still considered selfish to look after oneself, despite the fact that self-care has become commonplace. And on and on it goes.

I warned you it wasn't going to be a pretty start. A hypothesis was building. One I believed (at the risk of sounding great) could be an answer for others as well. Perhaps it could alleviate anxiety, agitation, restlessness, and dissatisfaction, sleeplessness, low-grade weariness, and tension, and hopefully more.

You see, what I'd previously discovered by delving into the 'ists' was that - surprise - we are neurobiologically programmed to belong. We know, physiologically, that we are wired for connection: to love and be loved. Love and belonging are critical for survival, let alone thriving.

How exciting. Here was a direct correlation demonstrating how hiding ourselves - striving to fit in by losing our identity - is detrimental to our overall health and happiness. Life becomes a fascinating but frightening loop: we conceal to fit in because we are programmed to belong, yet if we aren't truly belonging, we don't belong at all.

The 'ists' were arguing that we should seek love and security by doing everything we can to avoid being wounded or shamed. Perhaps we are stuck in perfectionism, comparison, activity, workaholism, or people pleasing. It's no surprise that many individuals feel fatigued and stressed. It's no surprise that the most common regret of the dying is this.

I now feel far less ridiculous for wanting to shake people at polite English social events and say, 'But what are you actually thinking?' or 'What excites you?' or 'What saddens you?' or 'Let's talk.' For wanting to rip my clothes off and go around among the supposedly tight ties and frocks, throwing creamy scones in people's faces and screaming! Obviously, I do not condone this! I understand that opening small talk is welcome, kind, and helps us feel safe with one other. But I'm the type who wants to pull back the curtain and see what's going on as quickly as possible. Take off your masks. See all the humanity. Both wonderful and ludicrous. Terrified and tremendous. Loveable and amusing.

## Waiting And Longing

It's strange how difficult waiting is. I've discovered that simply waiting for a bus can be really frustrating. Be still for a time. Feel the irritation. It's possible you'll feel uncomfortable. Oh how we despise feeling uncomfortable.

Waiting causes physical and mental discomfort to varied degrees, regardless of the cause - a late bus or the long-term loss of a loved one, a three-day migraine or ten years of disease. Waiting is difficult. It isn't a mild timeout. It is not a state of pleasure.

What time we will arrive at our destination, whose loved ones will accompany us, that employment idea, when we might become pregnant, or what our children will do. Of anything. However, we endeavor to retain control to alleviate suffering.

The discomfort produced by becoming aware of the depths of longing I had not previously felt was the most difficult blessing disguised as being forced to let up of control, sit in the darkness, and wait.

I did not want to be alone anymore.

I told myself that I wanted to find love and share my life with someone. I must say, MDRC, that admitting this was more difficult than I expected. Despite the fact that dreaming is exhilarating and necessary, acknowledging an internal need can be daunting. It's why so many people lose up on their dreams: it's difficult to accept what we don't have when we dare to wish. And in this scenario, I understood why the need to not be alone may be so strong: we are literally wired to love and be loved. To belong.

# Finally, Baggage Reclaim

I was nineteen years old and at the baggage reclaim area of Heathrow Airport after returning from months of touring around Australia and New Zealand. One of the most memorable and happy events of my life. The reason my memory of that otherwise tedious time in a municipally lit grey room - everyone fighting for their suitcases after a long flight among their weighty emotional baggage (pleased with that as well) - came to mind did not immediately present itself, but as I sat with it, it developed and became clear.

After collecting my well-traveled bag, I remembered sitting on a bench with grey, metal-backed benches rather than going straight to arrivals. They were next to the automatic arrivals doors, and my family was waiting on the other side to greet me and drive me home. I had begun to walk towards the doors, but just as they opened, I found myself plunging as if for protection into the seats. I hid. Something inside of me didn't want to return. As the recollection grew stronger, I remembered feeling confined - as if my true essence, which had been freed, allowed, expressed, and in flow while traveling, was returning to a place it shouldn't be or couldn't function in. I was rooted to the chair, thinking like a fugitive about how to flee. At the time, I had no idea why this was happening. I felt guilty since I had a loving family and a place to return to, but I was stuck at baggage reclaim and had no desire to return. It was as if my wild side was telling me that the plans I had for the future, the routines and habits of life that awaited me, were a trap and not who I was meant to be. I had no interest in studying politics at university in Bristol, which was my next move and one of the first micro-stabs I can recollect against my wild self. (I once read that it is the ongoing microaggressions rather than the major traumas that have a long-term impact on us.)

I have very few memories of my time at university, but I do recall traveling to London in the first term for a day-long interview for a stage manager course at Central School of Speech and Drama. I don't mind sharing; I finished first in my class and was offered a place. My immaculate presentation in a new hardcover binder at the Bristol Hippodrome, where I worked front of house, sealed the deal - nothing like laminating to impress. (I love stationery!) My enthusiasm for theatre had been with me since I can remember. I would have loved to go from politics to stage management. But I sat on the train back to Bristol, keeping the whole thing a secret, not wanting to rock the boat. (It appears a little mad to me now.) I didn't want to upset my parents or professors, and I was even shy about declaring I wanted to pursue a career in the arts. I hid my dreams and passions for a long time. I'm curious if the subtle ways we deviate from our nature cause mental and physical health issues and niggles. Perhaps it was no coincidence that I was returning to my parents' house before finishing my third year, having been greatly weakened by numerous diseases and viruses.

I'm not sure how long I was sitting at luggage reclaim. It seemed like hours. I recall stepping through the airport's sliding doors with a sorrowful heart. That nineteen-year-old realized, on some way, that in Australia, she was free since she was free of everything that might unknowingly enslave us.

If only we were honest. If only we listened. If only we knew what to do when we listened. If only we had the opportunity to act on what we've heard.

I was confident it was not too late. I could start anew.

I was off to reclaim her.

# Chapter 3: TREASURES

## A Silly Mood

I just made myself chuckle, imagining that those listening to the audiobook of my ramblings might think that the first treasure I discovered was the singer Cher. They might think, Wow, strange, she went through a torrid time and a key answer was pop sensation, nay goddess, Cher. Are we going to be instructed to ritualistically dance to 'The Shoop Shoop Song'?

Just to be clear to all of you listening half-heartedly to me while hoovering or driving (I jest, I love me an audiobook, and a hearty hello to you listeners), I mean 'share' as in S, H, A, R, E. Worth spelling out to us all, such is the importance of sharing. Not sharing everything, of course. I will not share food. Absolutely not. If anyone attempts to reach over and take a chip off my plate, they will be batted firmly away. Nor will I entertain the notion of 'can I just try yours?', and before I answer a fork is descending upon my plate. Absolutely not, thank you please. I chose what I'm having, you chose what you're having, and deal with it we must.

# A Problem Halved

That was an exciting bop! It transported me back to my school days. Always a happy location for me to visit. I realize I'm odd in that my school days were some of the best of my life. For years, I wondered why I missed school so much. In specifically, being a member of a sports team. It was where and when I was happiest: sharing a similar objective with my teammates and striving to improve ourselves with each other's aid. Nothing beats that.

What I've realized is that I was missing the genuine and profound connection that comes from being a part of a team. And that as an adult, I had unintentionally gone further away from that type of natural community and connection. I moved from being a reliable colleague to suffering the consequences of isolation. I became less and less practiced in communicating troubles (and perhaps this was never practised enough - an important thing we aren't often taught), or, rather, fully conditioned out of it, so that when my great crisis arrived, it was easier to keep the situation to myself.

I would be upset if I heard the phrase 'a problem shared is a problem halved'. It didn't make sense to me.

When we understand that the urge to be loved and belong is a vital element of our humanity, we also see that we are not helping ourselves when we do not connect deeply or share. It doesn't make it any easier, but knowing that it's what I need to do to remain healthy helps.

If we are intended to be loved and connected, not being heard is an assault on our identity. And we cannot be properly heard unless we disclose our issues. It's an attack on ourselves and our loved ones, to be honest.

My longing for the connection, camaraderie, and ready-made social life of my school days attested to this.

Indeed, there have been numerous research on the impact of loneliness, with strong evidence that it raises the risk of disease.

Why is it so hard?! Why did I get so riled up over 'a problem shared is a problem halved'? It seems strange to me now that I did, but the forces that made it easier to disengage were powerful.

Right, it was time to look at those forces, the habits I needed to break in order to reconnect and feel the health and goodness of being a teammate again.

## We Are Not A Burden

I'm using the term 'royal we' here, MDRC, since I'm confident that I'm not alone in fear of becoming a burden. I understand how easy it is to go it alone, having carried my own problems for many years.

It came out that I was more bothersome since I was afraid of burdening others! I was simply getting tireder, sicker, and more agitated by not sharing. When we refuse to let our friends and family in, they will become more concerned, not less. Unfortunately, refusing to ask for aid makes it more difficult to be loved.

And that's our response. We are wired to be loved, and connection is required to survive, much alone prosper, therefore sharing can be a terrible thought for us - what if we are rejected? The want for love and connection is so powerful that the fear of being without it makes it easier to hide.

People don't share because they are afraid of being misunderstood or condemned. Off we go, pretending we're fine so we don't burden each other. 'How are you doing?' 'Oh, very nicely, thanks.' "Are you sure... you're limping and your leg doesn't seem quite right?" 'I suppose I just broke it sliding down those steps, but I'll make a crutch out of a twig and get on with it; someone is coming for dinner, and I can't disappoint them. Onward and upward!'

If you, like me, desire data to back up the idea of the need to belong as part of our identity, there are plenty available, but I'd like to share my interpretation of the science, titled 'The Mess of a Break-Up'. Simply put, why do we shatter so quickly when we break up with a friend or partner? We really can crumble, can't we? I put it to you, MDRC, that if relationships weren't so crucial, we wouldn't fall apart. Royal Crumb Taster. Otherwise, I was just a woman in her forties listening to romantic melodies and snorting excessively into a crumble.

The sometimes craziness of breakups demonstrates to me the basic, human desire for connection. Although I briefly wondered why on earth I had even considered that greatest longing: to open the Hart heart to love. It felt incredibly vulnerable to explore romantic love after years of being single. Consider someone truly getting to know me, faults and all. (I do not have warts.)

The problem is that the longer we wait for it to connect in the proper way, the more difficult it becomes. Holding it together and not burdening others may appear to be a sign of strength, but being and feeling alone is quite frightening. What a sobering realization, MDRC, that we might be in biological, bodily stress when we are not frequently connected to someone who treats every aspect of us with respect and care. Disconnection is an unsettling experience, even at the cellular level.

When I realized that a felt sense of dignity was my right and what I need for a fully functioning brain and body, I began to believe I could reestablish a profound connection.

Of course, some individuals are born with vulnerability and sharing, and they understand that these are the foundation of wholehearted, healthy living; they simply will not comprehend those of us who are attempting to avoid being a burden. They may tell us, 'Yes, it can be uncomfortable and difficult to seek for help, divulge a secret, admit an issue, confront a relationship problem, or begin dating again, but what are the alternatives?' To which I would happily respond, 'Oh, that's easy, good old-fashioned emotional repression, keep calm and carry on, if you want a job done, do it yourself, being needy is weak and asking for help is embarrassing and pathetic, that is what the world has told us, so we are scared and scared to share, thank you please to you please!'

## To Vulnerability I Go

I was so removed from this element of my basic character, the want to belong, that I believed I had mastered vulnerability. When I met Jeremy Paxman, I burped loudly, not in revolt - I like him - but because one was brewing, and I didn't hold back. When I met the Queen, I told her, 'The pleasure is all yours, ma'am.' (A little awkward when she didn't realize I was joking.) It turns out that natural silliness and such pranks do not represent actual vulnerability.

MDRC, please bear with me as I reveal a harsh fact of discovery in this treasure: there is no getting around knowing and practicing vulnerability if you want to live a truly happy and free life. It's just not feasible. But, to encourage you, if it's something you need to work on for yourself, I'd like to tell you something very exciting. Drum roll...

I did it!

I soon learned to effectively express and convey what was happening to me, as well as to ask for what I needed.

Vulnerability meant that I told another person about some sad family news I had gotten while at work, and we both cried. It made it possible for her to tell me she was having panic episodes. We are still extremely close friends.

I begged to hold the hand of a well-known A-list Hollywood star (double vulnerability!) before we stepped on stage, explaining that I was nervous since I wasn't feeling well. I felt so much better expressing it that my nerves practically went away, and it pushed the other person backstage (who would ordinarily keep a high status) to reveal he was also nervous, and I then assisted him. Sharing vulnerably often liberates others. Helping others typically decreases fear.

I was happy to quit some of the little ways I hid, which can have a tremendous impact on our health.

As it dawned on me that I'd gotten isolated because I didn't know how to be vulnerable, I was looking forward to finally dispelling the notion that it was safer to go it alone or 'get it together'. To see that not allowing ourselves any weakness - whether it's basic exhaustion, a common cold, a difficult day at work, an emotional reaction, an issue we've let to grow and now feel ashamed about, or more severe illness or trouble - is simply nasty and stressful. It makes life difficult and scary for us.

Of course, we can be weak. In truth, "weak" is not the appropriate word. It has such bad connotations, despite the fact that it only indicates a lack of resources for a brief period of time. We're human beings in a challenging world, and we all have moments of 'weakness' when we need people and aid. Nobody is invincible. We are built to navigate our magnificent, incredible, and surprising lives, which will certainly include hardships, by connecting with ourselves and others. Admitting we are vulnerable when we are is a huge relief. More to the point, being vulnerable is by far the most powerful position to take. A superpower. What a relief, and how could the world have informed us otherwise? We do not need to have everything in order.

We are each vulnerable in different ways. Let us not forget that some people are vulnerable and feel threatened just because of their gender, race, or sexual orientation. Others could require financial assistance. Some people have less energy and require assistance with daily duties. Some people require help with their relationships. Some struggle with their self-esteem. Some require administrative assistance with their responsibilities. We all need assistance. Our vulnerability is what binds us.

It's simple to say now. It took me some time. I was fiercely independent, practical, and goal-oriented, so being incapacitated by illness was a major blow to how I had been living. I had been the stronger one. I could work long hours. I was professional and socially assured. I was also frequently the wise one, and paradoxically, I was always sought for and gladly gave advise. But being ill made me understand that I was also fiercely independent in a negative way: I didn't need people, I was afraid of being weak, and I armed myself with self-confidence and belief. I consider myself fortunate to possess some of these qualities. However, I've gradually worked on many of them, and I approach things in a more joyful manner. That is, while I am still confident and hopefully wise at times, I have come to realize that I will always be vulnerable and in need of others. I am more honest, and it is a huge relief.

'You may be vulnerable while still being powerful. You can have a kind heart while remaining rock-solid in your core. You can be mild as a wind and fierce as a dragon. The finest people usually embody both sides." - Author unknown.

If we just display our powerful or goofy sides, we can only form friendships on one level. If we show our friends everything, we will build a genuine, healing bond. It's easy to feel lonely even among friends if we haven't ventured to be open with them.

However, MDRC, choose your individuals wisely (or individually - we don't have to share with everyone). Ultimately, our minds and bodies want a sense of protection and dignity when we share with others. I discovered that a purposeful cuddle or a gaze in Peggy's eyes gave me a strong sense of affection.

All I can say is that when I allowed myself to discuss terrible experiences, my connections grew deeper and stronger.

No more brave-faced masks for me.

# Listen Up

Here's one major concern with sharing that I discovered and cannot overlook in our first treasure. And it is this: a culture that has not been educated to be vulnerable is not necessarily excellent at listening.

For starters, as we listen, we can go into repairing mode. I was a poor fixer who preferred to seek advice immediately. However, being fixed is not what we need when we share. My investigation revealed that it is often detrimental. It has the potential to promote the supposed anxiety that humans are innately flawed and require intervention. Trying to fix someone is not helpful or kind, unless that person specifically requests counsel. It's a short way to express that we don't have time for the other.

What we need, and why therapy can be so beneficial, is to be listened to without judgment. When we realize that another person is holding our circumstance with tenderness and love, it helps to alleviate our fear.

It's always worth sitting with our own unease while listening to someone openly share. They'll most likely be feeling awkward too. There we can find a clear and true friendship. We may be afraid of it, but we genuinely enjoy getting to know one another. As another nice man, Mister Rogers stated:

'To love someone means to attempt to accept that person exactly as he or she is, right now.'

# Gathering Onwards

Even in the midst of illness, I became really enthused about the prospect of renewing acquaintances. I knew my real, wild self was healthy when I was transparent and honest with a few close friends. Just thinking about it made me feel closer to the prospect of returning to myself. Genuinely, I would have swapped any previous success for actual connection. I had seen how aloneness can be really harmful to the body.

And I realized that the most essential thing was to continue exploring the cave for any treasures I might discover. There was no purpose in learning how to share and interact better if I was still exhausted and had a damaged immune system that prevented me from attending gatherings and parties. I still needed to discover answers about my health.

But it was exciting in the moment just to want to mingle in that larger context again. I've always enjoyed open, real, and fun socializing. In really heavenly timing, I came upon an episode of a podcast about 'the art of gathering'. It helped me realize that, in addition to losing the ability of listening, we've also lost sight of what it really means to gather. A gathering is an assembly or meeting, typically held for a specified purpose. That is the key—a purpose. For an event to engage us and make us feel pleased and present, it must have a clear aim.

How many times have you been nice and kind solely for the sake of being so? When a friend informed me she had to leave the phone because she was going to a party, I answered, 'Ooh, nice, have fun.' She said that she was dreading it. It was her neighbours' party, so she decided to sneak in, make her presence known, and depart as quickly as possible. I became pretty irritable! She became a bit of a headmistress. 'How would you like it if someone arrived at your party with dread and then snuck out as soon as possible? You are being rude and insensitive. She defended herself understandably, claiming that she did not want to be disrespectful by saying no. I mentioned that she was being even more impolite by going and leaving early after they had made such an effort, and that she could be concerned that she wasn't enjoying it. Plus, she was getting up early the next morning for a hard day and had told me how much she needed to relax. I pointed out that she was also lying to herself. She was being kind and kind for the sake of being courteous and kind, which meant she wasn't. By failing to show up on time, we abandon both our own and our friends' needs. I honestly believe that if we knew someone was going to meet us in those conditions, we would be extremely offended.

Unless we arrive to meet with love, having set aside that time for a specific reason, we are not acting honorably. For me, it's a return to 'clarity is kindness'. We confuse masks and formality with friendliness. I don't believe they are. Let's show up honorably, truthfully, or not at all. Hark at me!

I heard a story about a woman who was tired of the incessant small talk at the coffee mornings she attended with her school mom friends. She decided to be brave and propose that they change regular meetings into 'tea and tantrum' gatherings since she was fed up and tired and needed to vent. Everyone was relieved, and attendance skyrocketed with excitement and joy. They relished the opportunity to be authentic, and their moans inevitably resulted in much laughter and healing. They broke the courteous shine of tradition by gathering for a specific reason. I love it!

I am now very particular about any hosting I undertake. To the point where I provide a timetable for each occasion that resembles a party (I say party since it is usually limited to ten people with a pajama dress code). Everyone prefers to rest within a structure! It's simple to do when you host specifically - I might invite people over to watch something (Strictly Come Dancing is a natural example, or a fun film, or definitely sporting events), or I might gather for a sing-along (a yearly event for a group of us at Christmas), or for a celebration, a catch-up to encourage a friend, or a crafts session! And having a plan allows me to be extremely comfortable when entertaining since, for example, I've stated before guests arrive that I want them to leave by 9.30 p.m. so I can go to bed. Such freedom. At 9.25 p.m., if they appear too relaxed, I start saying, 'Open the Uber app, please!' My friend plays 'Climb Ev'ry Mountain' really loudly when she's struck a wall of overwhelm and wants others to leave. They know she's serious, so they all sing together as they walk to the door. Genius!

Surely we'd all prefer to connect with one another when we know why and how much we're helping? The vulnerability to gather for specified causes becomes enjoyable for everyone.

Are you motivated to join me for Treasure Two, MDRC?

Let us fortify with a dance break. It would be impolite to end this treasure without some Cher-ing... I'm going to Shoop Shoop again.

# Surrender

## Wasps vs Picnics

So I became energized about sharing, connecting, and gathering. I was on a fresh, exhilarating journey to release my wild side and forge forth. Then I was presented with the next treasure: learning to submit. Surrender? Umm. Doesn't sound very exciting. To put it mildly.

To be honest, MDRC, the early portion of the cave becomes a little foggy. But the concept of surrender startled me by becoming - actually - the unbreakable foundation for a peaceful, healthy life. It was critical for my health but applicable to many challenging situations.

Let me start with a light explanation. Imagine yourself sitting down to an ideal picnic. You've opened the Tupperware of small Scotch eggs (you're only human), have a delicious MOIST cucumber sandwich, and can't wait to get to the scones. Everything is amazing. And then a pesky wasp descends.

At this point, there are two options. There is the person who stays in the sandwich-eating posture and gently waves the wasp away, confident that they are unlikely to sting and will soon leave, and will not let it mar an otherwise lovely picnic. The other type of person (my hand has shot up again) will be immediately agitated - and possibly anxious - by the sight or sound of the wasp. They will begin doing what I call a panic waft, furiously trying to get it away because, frankly, everything was great and now look - everything is wrecked, typical! If a second wasp appears, this individual feels a sudden and significant threat and is on their feet, screeching and attacking an invisible monster with a napkin (the wasps had already flown in the opposite way). No one understands what they're doing; it could be a bizarre dance routine or they've simply lost the plot of life for a moment. As the sweaty napkin-waving-panic-wafter returns, the calm-carry-on-picnicking person has completed their sandwich, popped a couple of Scotch eggs, and is happily delving into their scone because they have cleverly placed a jam jar away from the rug so that any wasps will head in its direction.

How do they do this?!

Once, a wasp got too close to my cleavage, and I imagined it had dove down (since it has amazing cleavage) to sting me viciously on the nipple (imagine) or become lodged in another part of my garment. It was such an upsetting concept that I lost all moral or social compass and hastily removed all of my clothes to avoid a problem. The panic-wafter has been upgraded to panic-stripper. One minor issue: to my other picnickers, I appeared to be choosing to strip for them, as they had not realized there was a wasp in the mix. They were staring. I curtsied because it seemed the appropriate next step.

They've had a great time saving energy by not panicking or being irritated about the circumstance.

This is not a life skill that comes naturally to me. I lack the innate trust that things will simply 'work out'. I floundered when I became unwell and was unable to continue living my life only on the strength of my inherent fighting spirit. I attempted to resist the wasp. I wanted to fight my reality with everything I had, rather than face it. That's what we do; isn't it wild to struggle, repair, and force on?

Well, MDRC, neurology states, 'What you resist persists.' Sorry, but what? That sounded unpleasant to me.

What the hell is this?! I had to enter the gloomy portion of the cave.

# There's Nothing Wrong Here Right Now

As I continued to research the 'ism' on this topic, another sentence stood out: 'There's nothing wrong here right now.' WHAT?! It felt not only improbable, but also mean. Frankly, I would have struck someone in the face if they had said this to me while I was exhausted. I would have shouted, 'Excuse me, but everything is wrong! I am full of errors, so - and I mean this with no respect at all - GO AWAY, THANK YOU TO YOU!'

It turns out that the word actually means to accept what is. The intelligent 'ists' are stating that, despite being in a circumstance you would never pick, if there is nothing you can do about it at the time, you have no choice but to accept it as it is. And if you stop focusing only on what's wrong - on the wasp - there may be methods to make it bearable. Because, at the very least, you are already experiencing it. Like a true warrior. Many of us say, 'I can't do this,' or 'This is intolerable,' yet we do it anyway.

The 'ists' even argued that it is possible to arrive to the conclusion, 'Okay, this is what is meant to be happening in this moment, therefore I can accept and live it.' That's ninja-level magical calm, and I'm still amazed whenever I get close to it. All I know for certain is that with acceptance, much suffering can be alleviated. Or, more accurately, suffering about suffering.

They were not advising me to reject my circumstances or disease, but rather that if I approached it compassionately, rather than fiercely wanting it to go away, I might be able to find a way to accept it. The alternative was ineffective; every time I wished my symptoms would change, every time I complained about being bed- or housebound, I was merely exacerbating an already stressful situation. I'm frightening myself. It felt like I was continually viewing a horrible news reel.

Okay, I accept that the theory makes logic. Breathe and look around for some sliding kitties instead.

In retrospect, I see how exhausting it was to try to wish away a sickness. To constantly resist reality is, as speaker and author Byron Katie puts it, like attempting to educate a cat to bark. It would be gentler to accept what I was experiencing. Because we can only cultivate what we have right now. There is so much to succumb to. We cannot slow down time. We cannot change the landscape. We cannot change people. We cannot stop the aging process (not even by changing our appearance). We cannot change the weather, TV schedules, hardship, where we were born, or our natural abilities. And that's okay because that's how things are.

# The Twisted Ankle

I recall leaping enthusiastically into the BBC for a Comic Relief rehearsal; the event was going live on TV that night, and while I was always pleased to visit the BBC, live TV and Comic Relief heightened the enthusiasm. I wasn't exactly skipping in, but I might as well have been because I slipped on a bumpy section of pavement. When I tried to balance myself, I landed on the edge of a pothole and was soon on the ground, moaning in agony from going over on your ankle. Fortunately and shamefully, someone was passing by. They helped me up, and I staggered into the dressing room. I laid on a little two-seater sofa, my feet dangling over the edge (I hope it was tiny since it made me feel like a giant), my ankle hurting.

If I had the emotional agility, I would have surrendered to and accepted my transitory situation: I had a twisted ankle. Hey, hey. What can I do about it other than lie here and wait for the answers?

Instead, in a mature manner, I screeched, 'Well, this is blooming TYPICAL, isn't it? I won't be able to perform now, despite having worked so hard on this and having a strong desire to do so. Why are these things continuously happening to me? And, and … I was becoming healthy, and I won't be able to continue exercising now, life is so discouraging …' I went down that merry self-pitying mental tunnel.

In that moment, I was as comfortable as my long body could be on a small sofa. I was alive, breathing, and being cared for. Nonetheless, I chose complete grumpiness! Accepting the additional 'I'm letting everyone down' stress, as if it was my fault I'd sprained my ankle. Surrendering and accepting 'it is what it is' could have saved me a lot of worry, adrenaline, and negative energy.

Yes, it is official: I have always been a bit of a worrier! I wasn't going to berate myself because most people immediately react to adversity and try to maintain control. However, attempting to manage life is anxiety-inducing. I had no idea how much I had scared myself by attempting to manage things I could never influence.

Reflecting on my irrational reaction to the ankle, I realized that one key thing I wanted to improve was my negative reaction to things I didn't like or didn't believe should be happening. I wanted to move toward acceptance and surrender. But, at the moment, it felt too difficult. If I was like that with a twisted ankle, imagine being bedridden for years. I riled up like the best of them. I was a master at riling!

If I heard 'This too shall pass,' I'd immediately whisper, 'Oh, do shut up!'

If I read 'The way you feel today is not the way you will always feel,' I would sigh and say, 'Oh, now you "ists" are just stating the same thing in different fancy ways.' (I was, of course, addressing a book.)

This was the worst. 'Bloom where you were planted.' I answered, "Oh no, now please shut up once and for all." I'm blooming well but can't bloom, thank you very much. I'm far from blooming - I hardly feel like a seed, let alone a bulb that could bloom - so stop telling me I can bloom right now, since I'm completely bloom-less. This is a bloom-free zone!

## So, Why Is It So Hard?

Seriously, surrendering is obviously true, wise, healing, and the best way to make life simpler, so why did I find it so difficult? After speaking with some friends and family, I realized I wasn't the only one, so I was determined to identify the patterns we might be in that make it particularly difficult. I discovered two main causes.

The world has been shouting the contrary at us. Let me take this opportunity to remind you what I mean by 'the world'. I'm referring to modern society, the norms, practices, and trends we've been taught to believe are true. In this case, the yells read: keep going, never give up, push, push, push, do, do, do, achieve, and go, go, go. As adults, the busier you are, the apparently 'cooler' and 'better' you are: produce, enjoy, be joyful, party, and accumulate. I, for one, began to believe that was the wild, natural way to enjoy life to the fullest. I wasn't a workaholic, but I was definitely a productivity freak.

Many of us are hardwired to seek happiness: WE WANT IT ALL AND NOW! I particularly like philosopher Eric Hoffer's quote: 'The desire for happiness is one of the primary sources of sadness.' Feelings of 'I want things sorted and to be well NOW' and 'I just want to be happy' surfaced for me repeatedly. Exhausting. Of course, abandoning power would bring relief. Of course, there would be relief if my goal was to deal with what was going on in my life as best I could, rather than dwelling on any shortcomings in the pursuit of happiness.

THE WORLD SAYS fight, battle, push, fix, control, achieve, override, get out of the way of your feelings to keep doing, constant achievement should be celebrated, vulnerability is weakness, so hide your anxiety, stay upbeat and positive, striving is rock-solid healthy living, listening to your feelings and issues is a waste of time and selfish namby-pamby nonsense. Happiness is your goal. Success makes you a better person.

It seemed like a much better choice to follow the new method that was quietly spoken to me in the dark cave.

The truth is that acceptance, trust, optimism, self-compassion, and relaxation are the keys to finding peace and healing. Vulnerability is strength, and surrender is a place of transformation, a brave place to say 'help'. We were intended to be emotional beings. Life is up and down, darkness is permitted, and hardships are frequently excellent lessons and an essential part of living life to the fullest. Meaningful work is great if you obtain it, but what you achieve does not define who you are.

This brought me to the second reason. If surrender implies learning to remain still with 'what is', we may need to experience some - wait for it - emotions. Even the thought! I mean, as an actor, I can portray emotions, but in real life with my friends and family? Yuck! That truly takes the biscuit! (And frequently causes me to literally take the biscuit. "Eating your feelings, anyone?" We are not taught to sit with uncomfortable thoughts or feelings. All of the masks of fear, battling, repairing, busyness, and production have been used to conceal feelings and experiences that we do not believe we should have or display. It's no surprise that we're all so confused! However, we cannot change a situation unless we yield and accept it. Or cope with a situation. We cannot function from a position of strength while acknowledging vulnerability and seeking assistance. Instead, it is all too easy to critique ourselves and pass judgment on what is going on in our lives. When you think about it, that is simply mean!

Fighting and attempting to improve my circumstances, I understood, ultimately meant wanting my life and myself to be 'better' - some mythical best self who was superior to the real me now. So mean! The urge to be someone other than who we are can only be frightening and unpleasant. It is not a respectable or safe way to treat oneself, and our neurological system will respond accordingly.

So here I was, learning to tune out the yelling world and tune in to the newly relinquished frequency. Deep within, I knew this frequency to be true. But. The world's voice is incredibly loud.

I was in the place. It was completely engrained. I had always believed, 'I'm a strong independent woman; I can handle it.' It was as ingrained in me as a stick of granite that productivity was the key to pleasure. I repeatedly drowned out the new kind voice and continued to carry on.

# Facing The Monster

The most common reason we struggle to surrender to a painful situation is that we are 'simply' afraid of it. Of course we are, which is why it is causing us so much agony and anxiety. If we are scared of anything, we will naturally struggle and flee from it. Of course we do. It is our current enemy - our wasp, our monster - and we want to be rid of it. My monster was trapped by unclear and terrifying sickness symptoms (especially while waiting for a clear diagnosis). Others may experience anxiety, burnout, phobias, chronic tension, dissatisfaction, or a belief that they are not accepted for who they are. (The list might be limitless, unfortunately.)

I had to accept that the research was not only correct, but also the path forward; what you reject continues, and if you turn to 'face the monster', it will subside. It seemed really counter-intuitive. Such a difficult notion. To that end, the clinician from whom I learned, a brilliant 'ist' named John Gasienica, has put it in his own words to aid.

Now concentrate, MDRC; this is the therapy-ish part! But where can all the nice stuff come?

Our brain is continuously attempting to figure out whether the things around us are safe or dangerous. When we avoid something, we train our brain to predict that it is dangerous. If we ignore it long enough, our brain begins to categorize it as catastrophic, triggering a full-fledged dread response whenever we meet it.

Okay, that makes sense, John. It would be like me screaming at a precious, little child with my symptoms: "Yes, you should be terrified, this scenario is AWFUL, these symptoms and feelings are ALL WRONG, oh my God, did you experience that?"Be very scared, maybe we should go to the hospital, OH MY GOD, is that a wasp, RUN!" We would not do that. We would sit next to a fearful child, embrace them, and say, 'It's okay, I'm here,' and the youngster would automatically become more present and fearless.

John continues (we love John)...

The best method to improve our brain's threat prediction is to actively expose ourselves to what we're frightened of. If you are terrified of dogs, you can read all of the data demonstrating how safe they are. However, you will not be able to overcome your fear until you spend time with a friendly dog who sits on your lap. A corrective encounter occurs when you interact with something you previously feared and leave feeling safer.

It's a bit more challenging, John, but absolutely... I am with you... I do not want to be terrified of what I am going through.

When we continue to expose ourselves to the item we fear and have corrective experiences, our brain gradually loses the 'dangerous' label and no longer triggers a fear reaction. It frequently entails asking people to forgo their short-term comfort in order to feel safe in the long run. This is not an easy sell, but it is frequently required for recovery.

It's certainly not an easy sale, John. We still love you. And it makes perfect sense.

Something exciting happened in reference to the first two prizes. This seems apparent today, but it was a true aha moment. A great nugget! I discovered that it's no surprise that when we're asked how we're doing, we say things like, 'Yeah, fine, thanks, I'm fine,' when we're really not. How can we share if we haven't addressed and accepted our current situation? Or if we are ashamed of what we are feeling or how we are doing. (As an aside, I believe it is critical to show ourselves huge amounts of grace, even if we are unable to achieve what we know we should do. It takes us whatsoever long it takes.) My aha moment made me more motivated to surrender. I now know scientifically that saying I'm alright when I'm not makes me unconsciously more braced. If I'm not being honest with myself, all I can do is carry on.

I was glad to finally agree with the 'ists'. I was yielding to the concept of surrender.

# Crashed Again, But It Came Good

Plus, to be honest, I was given no choice. MDRC, my lovely body finally grabbed my attention after an attempt to return to work by collapsing (seriously) once more. Yes, I took one for the team to prove that soldiering on does not work!

I was very much bed-bound for another few months. Fatigue is difficult to express, especially since everyone gets tired from time to time. But it was back to the entire ghost-like frailty. I eventually started moving around, but a walk outdoors was as difficult as anything I'd done. I'd stand still on the road, as if I needed to remind my brain how to place one foot in front of another. I'd gaze at a cup of tea on the table and wonder if I had enough strength to take a sip.

I dreaded having to stare at this beast. I adored my profession, and knowing I wouldn't be able to continue with it was one of many heartbreaking moments for me. I recall hearing that kind and wise inner voice say, 'Who is to say that this isn't part of your tale, that good can't come from it? It's dishonest to try to keep glowing bright after your light has gone out. I was ready to get irritated and yell, 'Oh, do shut up,' but I didn't get sucked in (progress) and focused on the day's one work ahead of me: to take sweet Peggy for a short walk around the block. And in doing so, I learned something valuable.

I was shuffling down the street in a fog of exhaustion when I ran into the local dog walker and her gang of hounds. Peggy began yapping, fearful of the other dogs that had suddenly approached her. I wasn't paying attention and immediately sought to drag myself and Peggy away. The dog walker then mentioned something to me that I still think about.

'Your poor puppy,' she commented. I looked at her, puzzled. 'You need to reassure her, be the top dog, and educate her to follow you rather than drag her or let her run ahead.

Further benefit came from seeing that the anguish caused by this woman's misunderstanding was the same pain I was inflicting on myself by refusing to accept my situation. We effectively ignore, shame, misinterpret, and do not listen to ourselves. Pushing on is not kind. I was not going to fight anymore. No more carrying on for me.

## What's The Next Right Action?

When I first turned towards surrender, there was some choppy air (not only my personal wind - IBS was a minor concern - what do you mean I'm oversharing?) because that was the first time I had to deal with all of those emotions and needs.

In fact, brace yourselves - oops, wrong phrase; don't brace yourselves since it's terrible for your body and brain - and calmly accept what I'm going to say. I understand that many of us want to avoid our emotions or view them as monsters.

It is critical to go there since disregarding ourselves and our wants is detrimental to our health. None of us would sit back and allow an infected wound on our flesh to fester. You wouldn't look at the blisters, pus, and reddening and say, 'Oh gosh, that's so annoying, I have too much to do, I'll just put a plaster on it and get on with it.' No, you would be aware that you would soon be in severe pain and in a critical medical scenario.

But take one step at a time. I remembered a nice advise from a 'ist' (I was no longer shouting at them) who simply asked, 'Ask yourself: what's the next correct action in the present to move forward?' Instead of vehemently berating and evading, what is the kindest next proper action I can perform now that I've accepted reality? It may be confiding in a trusted friend or eating crisps while in the bathtub. The inquiry allows us to think about what specific items we might need help with. Einstein once observed, 'We can't fix problems with the same mentality that caused them.' It's a brilliant hack because we rarely consider that the correct next step is to panic!

For me, the next appropriate activity was, and continues to be, drinking tea or eating a snack. Always have a cup of tea and a snack... And in the weeks and months that followed the second fall, it was simply sitting at the window to absorb nature (with a cup of tea and a snack). Conceding to this restriction provided me with a unique opportunity to see the seasons. And it was settling, MDRC. I watched the weather, the clouds, and the leaves to remind myself that the only certainty we have is that things will change. It helped remind me that as I 'fronted the monster', aka my symptoms, they, too, would fluctuate, naturally rising and falling in intensity.

Nature appeared to move at a decent, steady pace. The earth was not rotating quicker, nor were the moon or the sun; it was only the world's system of over-productivity that was speeding up, and we were following suit.

Nature trusts the process. And one of the most valuable benefits of surrender is learning that any type of recovery is an ongoing journey. It could be recovery from a major event, such as a health crisis or a divorce, or something more little, such as a poor day or a cruel statement. We don't have to continually strive to control our surroundings and criticize ourselves for not doing better in each moment. We are a process. We are loved simply for existing.

The world's present pace was laughably attempting to overpower my nature, leaving no time for this process, my fragility, or my needs. (How many times have I said, 'I'll relax after I finish this' - can't it be just me?) It's no surprise that we're all so confused! And then, when things build up and monsters emerge, we may function from a frightening place of comparison and self-judgment since everyone else appears to be fine, so we put on our masks again, claiming we're fine and attempting to be acceptable. We've come to believe that despite our stress, we can't give up. Bless us. It's a difficult pattern to smash, but we must!

## Giving In Is Not Giving Up

Ah, giving in. I used to think this was nothing more than giving up. But that's a lie, MDRC. If we are even remotely confronted with our monsters, acceptance and surrender are not weak responses to a circumstance. The opposite. In this respect, fleeing is equivalent to surrendering. Meeting our deepest fears and confronting tough situations are undoubtedly infinitely braver than continuing or numbing out.

I've done some relatively bold things in my life. I've performed stand-up for 15,000 people at The O2. But, I declare, the most courageous thing I've ever had to do was accept how I felt physically and emotionally when I collapsed for the second time.

Allowing and accepting do not mean giving up. Giving up isn't really giving up. Quitting is often the correct, necessary, and gutsy thing to do. It's okay to take the wrong turn from time to time; who doesn't?

So here I was, confronted with my circumstances in order to forge a better path forward. My primary goal became to return to my wild, authentic self, to live freely and well.

John, our gorgeous 'ist', once mentioned that if I could closely observe an animal, I would notice that all they do is regulate themselves, become comfortable, and meet their needs. Always doing the next appropriate action. It was fascinating to see my dog closely and objectively from this perspective. Little Peggy was continuously altering her position to be as comfortable as possible. When she felt thirsty, she drank. When she wanted to go outside, she would let me know. After she ate, she rested, frequently taking two or three attempts to achieve the ideal position, twisting and turning into a tighter ball to get as cozy as she dared. Humans do not take as good care of themselves in their quest 'to do'. It's no surprise that we're all so confused!

It all comes down to the fact that my dog (and all animals) does not worry about her worth or judge herself based on how well she is doing or viewed; she simply knows she is a gorgeous, one-of-a-kind, amazing creature. It is her solemn duty to care for oneself.

# When You Are Waiting, You Are Not Doing Nothing

Sue Monk Kidd's When the Heart Waits is a richly honest memoir about her mid-life crisis. She noted in it, 'We gain our deepest development remaining still.' But my hand is raised again to say that it took this now-ex-productivity addict a long time to fully believe that.

I couldn't grasp - or trust - that my life would have guidance and direction, or begin to emerge, until I forced it. Without thinking about it, I'm planning and organizing to create a change for myself. But here's the amazing thing, MDRC: I discovered that when I stopped wasting energy to gird my loins and brace against reality, my body really began to heal.

The first profoundly essential element that arose for me was hope. I had enough energy to chose hope. It was still something I had to consciously choose. Eventually, hope grew, and I realized that even if I didn't completely heal, I could still have a wonderful life. I could handle illness nicely. I was no longer at odds with myself or my situation, and I realized that it was possible to achieve a serenity beyond all comprehension.

To stress, this was not a simple, laugh-a-minute experience. The only thing I could do comfortably from my bed or chair was watch movies, albeit I had to wear dark glasses at times due to neurological issues caused by light sensitivity. But hope meant that I could start seeking for the positive. A basic tool I learned was to do exactly that: Name the Good. If you're scared, look around you. Can you think of anything good? Nice colors in the room? Is there any beauty outside the window? This simple gesture might be transformative if we are locked in the negative mindset that nothing is good enough. Naming the positive (typically petting Peggy's velvety fur while drinking a cup of tea - not at the same time) was the way to maintain optimism, feel comfortable, and concentrate on the picnic rather than the wasps.

But that was pretty much it. Nothing more marvellous or miraculous (but it seemed like both). I just decided not to put on a brave façade any longer. I felt quite unwell, so I would simply let myself be. I felt weak, so I allowed myself to be so. I was terrified, so I let myself be. It was not easy. As a result, a sense of relaxation emerged.

Acceptance and surrender are the most powerful actions you can perform when you need to. Surrender marks the beginning, not the conclusion. It is the foundation of transformation, from which all good things emerge.

# Feel, Grieve, Let the Past Be the Past

## Goodbye, Peggy

When my beloved-beyond-all-compare dog Peggy died, I experienced a level of anguish I had never felt before. I was emoting, sharing, expressing, and sobbing - openly. I discovered that the death of a pet is understandable and acceptable. That being said, it was unexpected to see my dog's death in the broadsheet headlines! I could have been humiliated, but I saw it as a testament to our canine friends' great power.

Peggy taught me many lessons throughout her life, as dogs do if you let them. It's part of their job, along with showering us with unconditional love and loyalty (and, of course, teaching us how to clean up poo in one swift motion). They do so with grounded simplicity. Without a spinning human brain, they are able to be present for the one thing on their doggy to-do list: following their person about and showing them they adore them. At all times. You can share experiences with a human friend, but you never know if they're thinking about what chore they have to do next or what they're worrying about. A dog is fully present, with no such concerns. I was instantly calmer, breathing better and slower, and the absence of resistance to what was happening allowed my body to recover. To that end, Peggy was probably my first teacher in surrender and acceptance.

It wasn't until the first few days, when the sadness was hammering so hard, that I realized the pain was from losing that loving presence in its most pure form. My grief was exacerbated by guilt over not being as present with her as I could have - and really wanted to have been - in her final months. I had gotten obsessed with the illnesses I was battling. I had allowed disease to become my identity. Disaster.

The first morning after she died, I would have given anything to have her back and experience the classic enthusiastic Peggy morning greeting (even if it involved a paw plant right on my nose before I had really woken up). I'd give her a quick brush and a grin lately; I'd never neglect her - she was too lovely to ignore - but I'd take her for granted.

The regret of wishing I had spent more time just caressing her, lying next to her, was a tremendous wake-up call for me to realize that I had been stressing about how unwell I was and thus getting sicker. I was missing the car rides and how much I adored her sleeping in the passenger seat or staring up at me while I sang my heart out! Finding a grassy verge at the service station to pee on—her, not me. All the routines. Many of them we had not done in a long time since my dear body was unable to. We had rarely been separated. I missed her sleeping near me while I wrote.

Walkies were equally exciting for me and her. With a dog, you feel spiritually connected to your animal's joy in their surroundings. Your heart races as they look around to see if you are still with them. Always linked and never too far apart. My last proper country stroll with Peggy was years before her death.

Peggy's passing prompted me to confront all I had been mourning due to illness. The realization of this, while painful, was the first step toward healing. Perhaps she departed to catch my attention.

It certainly brought to light the fact that grieving the loss of a pet was the first time I had honestly expressed myself - and been heard - in a long time. This, in turn, brought to light the fact that I hadn't grieved my full diagnosis, which I had been looking for and ultimately received a few months before Peggy died. After the diagnosis, I sniffled for a few days before instinctively returning to 'stay calm and carry on' mode.

Why was I allowing myself to grieve for Peggy while remaining silent about my diagnosis? If I considered trying to cover up Peggy's death, I felt the old bracing tightness around my muscles. It's bad enough when you need to cry but can't and a tight lump forms in your throat.

It was easier to handle my grief over Peggy because I could discuss and express it. My heart mended relatively soon. But why hadn't I done the same with my diagnosis, despite the frustrations of illness? This jewel held the answer for me. MDRC promises that the treasures will become more playful and tranquil, though the situation remains unclear. In fact, 'peace' has become my watchword for our third treasure together.

The only way to get there was to pass through the darkness.

## Do I Have the Right To Grieve?

I realize now that I didn't feel I had permission to grieve my diagnosis, in part because I was acutely aware of my privileges - I had to tell myself that there is no way to quantify what makes one person's sorrow worse or better than another's. According to grieving specialist David Kessler, 'What each person is going through is the hardest thing that they have ever been through.' Everyone has the right to grieve.

A question was formulating. What if we become trapped in some illnesses and situations because we lack the ability to grieve and feel them, or because we refuse to do so? We're not letting them pass through us. Umm …

## All Hail The 'Ists'

Sure enough, all of the 'ists' on this subject reminded me that if we don't honor and release our sorrow, scars, upsets, and disappointments, we will just repeat them. Ignoring and pushing away what we consider to be painful feelings is so entrenched in us (at least in me). Instead, we force the good. However, strategies for avoiding discomfort are ineffective. That energy of feeling (emotion is energy in motion) may be suppressed, yet it continues to bubble away in the body, unreleased.

As trauma expert Bessel van der Kolk wisely stated, "The Body Keeps the Score." Is it any wonder that so many individuals have fatigue, tight shoulders, jaw discomfort, headaches, lower back pain, and migraines? It's not simply a lack of an ergonomic chair and computer setup; many of us are clinging on to retain a good appearance. Wearing masks allows you to avoid being criticized or unloved for experiencing feelings that the world considers less acceptable.

For years, I was opposed to feeling anything other than happy and positive. It turns out, MDRC, that this is neither human nor scientifically conceivable. Apparently - and I apologize for hitting you with this since I didn't want to hear it at first - if we suppress one end of our emotional spectrum, we must suppress the rest. We wind up in a dull middle ground.

If there is physical discomfort, persistent troubles, disturbed sleep, digestive problems, or dissatisfaction, there is probably a tender little feeling rumbling around that has to be released. If only we could fart out our emotions. Ironically, that is one thing I freely release.

So there you have it. It certainly is better to be outside than within. All the 'ists' argue that what comes out of you does not make you sick; it is what stays inside that does. I was starting to consider the possibility that some of my ongoing ailments were related to emotional repression.

# 'Don't Get Emotional, We're Not Spanish!'

That was a line delivered by the upper-class mother character in the first episode of my sitcom. It was a rather apparent technique to assist the audience comprehend her persona, but Patricia Hodge's delivery made it incredibly humorous. It's possible that only a British audience can completely grasp it; other people become sick just thinking about having an emotion! Many people were raised to be quiet and polite at all times. That being noisy in any way is inappropriate.

So, for those who thought this foolish statement was a dig at the Spanish, think again. I'm sure this is why Italians may be able to eat spaghetti and pizza while experiencing fewer heart attacks. They can argue, express their feelings, gesture irritation, and then laugh and hug the next minute. They let it out. That strikes me as natural and true. There's an authentic wildness to it that you don't always see in Britain. I should emphasize that the line was not intended to mock our British uptightness. There is much to admire about our tenacity, duty, and ability to remain cool and carry on. Often, these are necessary and noble characteristics. However, this does not always happen.

However, we cannot simply tell someone with culturally established, buttoned-up emotions, 'Come on, just let it all out.' As I looked into the 'ists' on this treasure, I realized it would require some learning and unlearning. Many patterns to smash. Ready to jump in with me, MDRC? Begin to sense some emotions? Don't worry, I had to go very softly. So much so that I began by explaining what an emotion is. If you're frightened, try singing 'Jerusalem' or the national song while grabbing a Victoria sponge. Soon it will be a piece of cake (thank you).

## What Is A Feeling?

Feelings are the conscious responses to emotions. Stick with me, MDRC; I found this quite helpful in learning. Emotions are subconscious energy - raw, direct reactions to the present situation. (I mean, I didn't know that; what a revelation.) Allow me to illustrate with an example. If someone hides behind a door and jumps out at you, you will most likely scream instinctively. When you are startled, you may rush out of the way, put your palm over your mouth, feel shaky, heated, and flushed, as you recoil from what your brain cleverly immediately perceives as a danger. All of the energy in motion originates from the primordial part of the brain that protects us. That is emotion. Pure physical energy can be represented in a variety of ways, including physically, facially, with noise, and through words.

Now, keep focused on my lesson, MDRC, as it becomes more interesting and useful. Emotions impact our feelings, but they also stem from our cognitive thinking. Feelings are the meaning we attribute to an emotion. Don't you find that fascinating? I pondered why I hadn't realized it sooner. As a result, feelings may become stories we make up about past experiences or future anxieties. For example, if my friend leaps out at me and I scream and am startled, I may feel cheerful, fun, and delighted because I enjoy surprises, and having a dynamic connection helps me feel appreciated. The initial shock and scream transforms into sweet sensations of laughing and connection. However, for another person or on another day, receiving such a shock, together with the energy that emotion generates, may result in feelings of anxiety, upset, or tension. It might remind me of anything from the past, intentionally or unknowingly, and my friend might see it as a nasty deed rather than a humorous, loving one. These are the feelings that result from emotion. All this happens in the blink of an eye. I pondered why any of us had grown so fearful of or disconnected from this aspect of our humanity. This is extremely important to know. So natural.

Emotions are the body's fundamental, instinctive, and subconscious responses to the present moment. Feelings are our mental thoughts about an emotion, not the reality of the circumstance. Okay, that explains why people get trapped.

But we are emotional beings, and we cannot thrive without them. We need the energy of fear, for example, to leap out of the way of a speeding car. We are emotional beings; otherwise, we have no significance. We are feeling beings with meanings (this felt like a tiny rhyme). We can't stop feeling. It is impossible. We might as well discover them, become acquainted with them, and learn how to cope with them, wouldn't we? Even enjoy them.

They are part of who we are. They enhance the beauty and richness of life. They are honest. I believe that everyone should have the freedom to be themselves. I was motivated to continue digging.

First, I'm going for a dance break. Because, of course, you make it happen with your passion and dance your way through life. It's always funny to speak music lyrics.

# Childhood

Welcome back, MDRC. I'm pretty sweaty. That was quite a routine. I frequently consider charging for entry to my house dance parties. There would be a rush for tickets due to the gay abandonment of my performing style and the rogue and revolutionary usage of props. I just performed quite the maneuver with a laundry basket. Moving on...

It's a deeper look into the emotional realm.

Here we go with a deeper dive. We cannot deny that at some point in our lives, we were all children. (Do not claim you don't learn from me.) We all, regardless of our current status on Earth, were once small, frail naked babies. Forgive me, MDRC, if you're picturing Putin in nappies. Forgive me if you weren't picturing Putin in nappies before, but now you are, which is the most likely situation.

We all began as vulnerable, delicate, little beings with the capacity to evolve into the loving, uniquely created beings that we are now, and how we were reared, what we witnessed in our first few months and years, will have a significant impact on our future.

This was likely one of the most eye-opening and significant revelations I had in this metaphorical cave I was wading through. To survive, we require a loving relationship to a caregiver who will feed, clothe, shelter, provide physical touch, demonstrate love, and gently guide our early development. As our brains mature, we require a caregiver to help us feel safe so that the survival part of our brain, which produces dread for crises, does not become locked in that state. To develop a healthy neurological system, we must be loved and approved of throughout our lives in order to feel safe. We need to feel safe enough to set boundaries, learn to say no, and express ourselves. The difficulty is that not everyone enjoys that security; according to one statistic, half of the world's population suffers from problems caused by a lack of protection throughout early growth. Whatever it is, for us to survive, we must adapt quickly. This is incredible information, MDRC; we are programmed to appease our caretakers in order to safely attach to them. If that means being silent and not sharing how we feel, we've found that when we do, we get attention, shut up, and possibly shut down. If we exclusively show our parents our accomplishments because that is how they praise us, we may establish a cycle of perfectionism. If we try to be as helpful as possible while ignoring our own needs, we may acquire people-pleasing tendencies.

It was a fascinating, lightning-bolt moment for me to realize that we are all dear children who had to adapt to feel safe and loved, and that sometimes that adaptation is unhealthy and is encoded into us throughout our adult lives.

To summarize the heavy revvy (heavy revelation) of this treasure: if we suppress our feelings to fit in and be loved as children, it's initially a very clever approach to find security, but if we carry it into adulthood, we'll remain trapped in a subconscious pattern of fear. Our brains preserve our early attachment memories; there's nothing wrong with being apprehensive or stuck in patterns you don't want to be in; it's not your fault. In truth, you were an incredible child who learned to live. Well done, MDRC. Furthermore, the 'ists' told me that we could destroy the old unproductive patterns. Yay, and phew!

## The Girl Who Was Scared Of the Dog

Regardless of how excited I was about all of this learning - since I was confident it would relate to my physical health difficulties - I needed to take regular breaks (sometimes days or more), which would allow me to reminisce on moments with my beloved Peggy. I recall sitting on a bridge across a little brook when a couple with two young children approached. Dear Peggles raced up to them with a short yelp and made a beeline for the older child, obviously wanting to hug. Though the smaller child went forward to play with Peggy, the elder child clutched her mother's hand, recoiling when Peggy leaped at her face.

Then her mother abruptly exclaimed, 'You can't possibly be terrified of this tiny fluffball, I mean honestly!' I don't think she was annoyed with her child, but rather embarrassed by her at worst. But those remarks cut me as deeply as they did the girl. She shrank in stature, turned aside, and obviously wanted to cry.

There it was. The mere act of invalidating a child's fear might lead to further fear.

We are frequently more afraid of feeling the emotion than of experiencing it.

Little child, I'm curious where you are today. Please know that you had every right to be terrified of Peggy. If a dog my height sprang up in front of me and I hadn't been told it wouldn't bite my nose off, I'd probably scream and never go outside again. I believe you were more wise and fearless than your younger sister, who went towards a weird ball of fluff. Nothing was wrong with you, little child.

# 'What's Not To Be Happy About?'

That little child being forced to smile despite Peggy's meaty breath in her face was also a therapeutic illustration of the next thing I learned from the 'ists': 'toxic positivity'. Another lesson is coming, MDRC.

The society in which I grew up meant that if I revealed a brief piece of my worry or frustration, the answer was usually 'chin up', 'keep going', 'look at all you have to be glad about', or 'you're okay, it'll be great'.

'Go and grab the day', 'be optimistic', 'be nice', 'be brave', and 'take on the world' are all positive statements. However, when they prevent us from experiencing a complete emotional experience without shame, when we are more concerned with letting the mood down, not being liked, or being a burden, we are establishing a toxic positive culture in which suppression is the only option.

How exhausting is it to constantly have to be 'on form'? That seems like a cage to me. What does it mean, anyway? Surely, 'on form' is simply how we are and who we are, and this will change from day to day as our experiences influence how we react to situations. Some days I may be quieter and more reflective, and that is fine.

I will always be a sensitive person. I get startled quickly and have a strong imagination, so if I'm swimming in the sea and something brushes against my skin, I'll scream and imagine it's a poisonous snake, even if I'm in England, where there are none. It's usually a stick, a plastic bag, or, at worst, a piece of seaweed! I'll cry with excitement by the sight of a puppy leaping or a sunset. My heart fills when someone I care about feels encouraged and proud of themselves. I cry. Then hop up and down. And then wee. When someone surprises me, I get apprehensive and eager (you have to know me really well to pull off a surprise that works).

Was I informed that I'm too sensitive? YES.

Am I overly sensitive? NO, no, no, and all other noes in the Kingdom of No.

It is who I am. It's how I'm created. I can't change it. I don't want to break down in front of someone who has just seen me on television. I would rather not. To that end, in light of my diagnosis, I realized how exhausting it would be for those already struggling energy cells to conceal my sensitivity.

# Stuck In The Mud

I grew stronger a few years following my diagnosis. And one day I had enough energy for a trip to the beach. I can't tell you how magnificent the sea appears after years of being inside. A friend and I leased a kayak and a small RIB boat with an engine (for paddling breaks) for a leisurely paddle up a gorgeous creek. It was peaceful for a little while until the engine on the small boat, which was also towing the kayak, died. The tide was swiftly receding, and we knew that returning to our jetty against the tide and wind, as well as the estuary's deep, sinking mud, would be difficult. We attempted to use the kayak paddle to propel the boat, but we were making no progress - that is, we were staying static and moving backwards despite our best efforts. We were up shit creek with the incorrect kind of paddles (not sorry about that). It was time for me to get into the kayak and try to tow us in (it was a single-person kayak, regrettably). What I assumed would be a straightforward transition from a RIB boat to a kayak WASN'T. I did not make a solid move and plopped into the water (screaming at the'snakes'!). You eventually lose your Crocs. My companion was hysterical, but I was not! I couldn't get a good grip on the kayak as we were gradually dragged back down the creek. I kept telling my friend, quite seriously (which made her laugh even more), 'Stop laughing, it's not funny till I'm in!' I was glad to find the comic side of this trip, but I was afraid and out of breath (this was quite the excursion for someone who had just been bedbound and was still experiencing the odd PoTS attack!), and I needed some type of safety before I went.

I offer this tale because it helped me understand that we adult people, just like our loving young selves, need to feel protected. That is often why we do not express our emotions. We don't feel comfortable in our environment. We need the right people, as well as a sense of belonging and self-esteem, to feel and express our emotions.

# Feeling Good

Sometimes it feels like you're fighting upstream, against the flood, as you negotiate feelings you've buried for years, as you realize why you suppressed them, and how and why you need to release them. But, in general, all I can say is that I expected it to be much harder than it was.

Although this is not a 'how-to' book (I plan to create an accompanying workbook), I wanted to offer a few ideas that I found useful in case you're going through a difficult time, MDRC.

The first thing to remember is that you are a human (don't say you don't learn from me), and humans have nervous systems that require a sense of safety. You could conclude that I was naturally trusting of The Boy. But I also had to learn to build that safety for myself. If I kept pretending that everything was fine when it wasn't, I'd be lying to myself, which lacks respect and kindness. The 'ists' all agree that a sense of safety builds with growing acceptance, as you approach your suffering and sensations with kindness. I was overjoyed I had done it with The Boy. Instead of worrying about being regarded as a diva, lazy, or weak for allowing him to make me tea on our first date at my place, I addressed my own physical exhaustion. I could feel my body relaxing as it realized it could start to trust me. An absolute must for chronic illness recovery.

I also kept reminding myself that the individuals I admire and love, whose tales inspire me the most, are those who truly GO THROUGH THINGS. I never consider someone who is experiencing darkness to be weak. Quite the reverse. It crushes my heart when people with anxiety and chronic diseases see themselves as weak. Those that have to deal with chronic diseases are frequently the most resilient in terms of getting up and moving. I nearly apologized for getting on a soapbox, but I'm feeling what I'm experiencing, and it feels amazing!

# Do Look Back In Anger

A separate note on rage. For me, it was one of the most difficult sentiments to befriend. Could I trust my anger? Could I allow myself to be angry, especially after being told it was a 'bad' emotion and looked horrible on women? I knew I had to destroy that horrifying pattern. I was undoubtedly angry about my decades-long misdiagnosed. Of sure, we might be furious over what occurred to us. Anger is often a necessary or appropriate response. Frequently, anger must precede forgiveness. Without rage, little happens in the world. Without rage at pain, compassion cannot emerge and prevail. Of sure, we can be furious about what the world does to others. Go to the top of a hill and shout, scream into a pillow, or sit alone in your car and let it all out. Whatever you need. I was a cushion pummeller (not a euphemism). Anger releases you from the past. Bit by bit. It motivates you to move forward and make changes.

I realized that exhaustion, lethargy, and indifference are frequently the manifestations of trapped fury. I was shocked at how often my exhaustion lifted when I vented my frustration, either verbally or physically (my poor cushions!). The mind-body connection was proven instantly. I wasn't terrified of anger any longer. I was more afraid to hold it in.

## Everything Is Bigger In The Wild

When I was obliged to explore the world of well-being, I came across some unusual proposals and practices. Some of them were easy for me to dismiss, such as bee venom therapy - oh, NO, THANKS! - and fish pedicures - STOP IT! I always require at least some science or a solid foundation. That is why I will not rush into reiki and the like. I will also refuse to perform things that are likely to be beneficial to you simply because I dislike them. When someone first suggested that I do tai chi, I launched in: 'I mean, with all respect' - by which anyone usually means no respect at all - 'it's just that kind of **** that puts everyone off trying to feel better because they see people wafting their arms about and having a green smoothie and a bit of fun, and that's all very well and good if you feel okay, but when you're seriously unwell, you actually need something a bit less **** than tai ******* chi.' Though I wouldn't call this an excellent example of emoting toward a fellow human, I'm only trying to make a suggestion!

And two months later, I'm having the time of my life at a tai chi lesson! I now practice tai chi on my own from time to time, often turning it into a form of ballet to entertain myself. (It's all about discovering what works for you.) Tai chi showed me something quite unexpected. But it was taking up my entire sense of space, being truly seen, and physically there that made me shy. As a performer, I was astonished by my response.

But it was quite a revelation. Tai chi provided me with the information I needed to break free from a detrimental childhood pattern: the younger me believed (rightly or erroneously) that she should be quieter, not disrupt the calm, not seek for help, and just get on with it. Now I understood I wanted my adult/wild self to believe she could be as big as she naturally should be.

# Rewilding

When I first visited Knepp in West Sussex, a 3,000-acre estate that has been left to rewild itself for the past twenty years, I was astounded by the effect. When I walked through the gates, something shifted in both the environment and me. Even only a short way from the gate, the environment had changed dramatically. The rewilding had created a 1,000-year-old England, which was both ancient and entirely new to me. I was still in Sussex. I could occasionally hear the buzz of the A24. There were oak trees, birdsong, and other things I'd grown up with, yet it was utterly different. I stood still, stunned. I was amazed not just by the surroundings, but also by how light I felt. It's difficult to explain, but everything in Knepp appeared more bright and alive, and I felt it myself.

On my first night, I went for a walk about dusk. Everything around me was chaotic, everything seemed larger, and I felt smaller than before. Nonetheless, I could firmly take up my spot. I was in a big environment, and I knew I belonged and could fit in. There will be no whacking of furniture if I do a Tai Chi move here!

Everything is bolder, brighter, and more lovely in the wild. And once we're wild again, we're at ease. The irony is that our fear of our wildness is frequently what keeps us trapped. We don't want to draw attention or upset the status quo. But it is what we must do. Do not be afraid of your wild side. You wouldn't stop a lion from screaming, a youngster from laughing uncontrollably, or a tree from blooming. It would be quite mean. Don't try to fit in, since you are beautiful in your wildness.

It dawned on me at sunset that it always comes back to trusting in one's fundamental identity. Surely, if we knew we were completely loved, we could express our emotions without fear of being judged? If we could trust that we are at our most exquisite when we let ourselves go, sentiments would undoubtedly exist as a glorious and exciting aspect of our existence.

I was no longer going to keep it all together. Not all illnesses are caused by stored emotion, but many are; it is what our bodies do. They hold all of our experiences. It's simple science, and no matter where you are on the spectrum from dis-ease to disease, living completely human means being totally present to your emotions and feelings.

I no longer feel like I'm failing myself at previously perceived lesser emotional moments.

In fact, I feel as if I have failed myself.

# The Fire Pit

You see, MDRC, I didn't understand until Peggy died that my identity had been almost entirely focused on my health. It looked like the proper thing to do at first, as part of the solution-finding process (of course, the reverse was true). After discovering what I had with this treasure, I wanted to create and memorialize a moment to commemorate my turning the ship from the past. To celebrate becoming less of a wallowy old hippo! I wasn't completely cured by any means, but I knew it would be a step toward that goal.

I had a file filled with old medical records. And a box full of old journals. I took them into the garden and started a little fire in the fire pit. I took a quick peek at some of the medical files and noticed TATT at least three times in scrawly writing. I observed endless blood test results and doctor's letters indicating my elevated inflammation levels and the frequent activation of glandular fever, but assuring me that it wouldn't be an issue. I burst into tears as I realized how many months and years I had lost due to illness.

I dared to peep inside my journals. Some date back to 1991. Although there were some amusing entries, particularly about Jason Donovan's forgotten love and a strange fascination with Harold Bishop and Mrs Mangel from Neighbours, it was mostly a repetition of why I couldn't do what everyone else could, how I was going to feel better, the worry of always disappointing friends, and so on.

It all ended up on fire.

As I burnt papers and journals, I honored my tale with pain that I hadn't allowed myself to feel at first. (I was genuinely Spanish!

I didn't have Peggy by my side, but since I'd learned to accept my emotions and watch them pass, I was able to create a secure, loving presence for myself. I could trust myself to handle whatever life had in store for me. And that gave me calm.

# Thoughts

## Home And Away

Back in 2013, a few years before the terrible disease business had taken over my life, I was still working and travelling. There was never a full tank of energy, and I was beginning to experience more serious symptoms (and injuries), but a collapse was still a long way off. I feel my passion for my profession and the individuals involved kept me going. I have a unique memory from that period, so please join me in returning to 2013, MDRC.

It was February, and I was lying on a beach in Australia, resting before my stand-up act that night. Not just any beach, but Palm Beach, the location of the Home and Away filming! Oh, I had the Surf Club there in front of me. Not only was it the set of a TV show I used to enjoy (obviously I had a slight fascination with Australian soaps …), but I was laying in the exact position I had been twenty-one years ago, on my travelling experience. Everything remained the same: the eternal waves, the offshore breeze, the almost-orange sand, the grassy banks above the beach, the blazing Australian sun, and even the trailers, trucks, and crew people signaling that Home and Away was still in production. Even the actor who portrayed Alf! (Perhaps it was a huge obsession. Let us not dwell.

Everything was the same for me, except for the effects of twenty-one years of living. The experiences it brings, the suffering it endures, the dreams it realizes, the unfulfilled dreams it ignores, the wisdom gained, and the innocence lost. Despite all of the changes, I still felt the same way at my core. I now understand that our inner self - that wild, natural person with our distinct personalities, skills, and characteristics - remains constant. However, in adulthood, it is buried behind roles, responsibilities, and so-called worldly norms.

At the age of nineteen, I was a thin and fit athlete in Palm Beach. I was a dreamer who was really present in the moment, exploring, engaged, and expressive. I was loud when I wanted to be, but quiet when I needed to be. I was free of the necessity for a specific path or vocation to follow. I was free of the necessity to wear make-up or conform to a fashion or dress code, as well as the burden of a packed social calendar. I wasn't looking for hobbies because I was already doing everything I enjoyed. Due to financial constraints, I survived on Vegemite sandwiches, yet I never felt hungry. Similarly, sharing dorms in youth hostels or sleeping in corrugated-iron-roofed shelters close to service stations in the outback. I slept well. Inadvertently, I was doing what I needed to do to live a healthy life: on purpose, in connection, in the moment, inspired and delighted, joyous and playful, and exercising simply by doing what I enjoyed every day. I was not swayed by decisions or choices that did not reflect my ideals.

## At Home With Thoughts

It was a welcome break from the dark tunnel of disease to be back in the sun, sand, and space of Australia (in my imagination). It was also nice that I knew my nineteen-year-old self would agree with me now that our biggest ambition is to be at home with our thoughts, free and confident in our own skin. Isn't that everyone's dream?

This then inspired me, MDRC, to become aware of any thoughts that may be causing current misery (also, I didn't want to have another list of useless worries to write myself in twenty-one years). I already knew from the 'ists' that it is typically the thoughts about circumstances that create the most pain, not the conditions themselves. To that purpose, I investigated if ideas could be analogous to the effects of emotions on the body. Certainly, by continuing to surrender to symptoms and expressing my sentiments about the disease I was dealing with, I was making some physical progress. I was ready to dig and go further in the hopes of discovering more secrets about the mind-body link. To heal. In your face, Lyme disease and your horrifying related conditions!

# What Are Thoughts?

MDRC, we are extremely fortunate to live at a time when cutting-edge neuroscience confirms what spiritual wisdom and teachings have taught us throughout history. We now know - and it's MIND-BLOWING, MDRC (pun completely intended, and I doubt it will be the last time I say it) - that ideas are real matter. They consist of proteins and substances. Yes, our thoughts are real things. So, if we continually align with negative thoughts, they will become stronger, establish long-term memories, and trigger a toxic-stress response. Basically, what we think about grows. MIND-BLOWING. Every cell in our body is affected by our brain chemistry, thus toxic stress from negative thoughts can cause discomfort, inflammation, and disease. Wow.

We also now understand that the mind is independent from the brain. Whaaaat?! MIND-BLOWING. That means our mind - our will, decisions, habits, and every idea - influences our brain. Our thoughts either grow into healthy, nourishing trees in our brains, or they do not. Our brain is the body's powerhouse, housing the immune, neurological, and hormonal systems. A healthy brain is necessary for a healthy body. As a result, as all of the 'ists' claim, separating mind and body is illogical and scientifically impossible.

Wow, again. So every anxiety or aggravation about my physical situation exacerbated it. For all I knew, there could be a reason why it was perpetuated. This was already a dazzling gem from the cave wall.

And three times, wow. That is, subconscious negative thoughts may have diluted my wild self. Oh, I was not going to have any more of that, thank you very much. I did not want to operate under any form of dread, especially not inadvertently. I felt even more energized.

I found this incredibly helpful quote from Buddhist teacher Yongey Mingyur Rinpoche in his book In Love with the World: 'The less we know about the chattering, muttering voice in our heads that tells us what to do, what to believe, what to buy, which people we should love, and so on, the more power we give it to boss us around and convince us that whatever it says is true.

And a fourth wow to that, because I want to be the boss! I did not want any hazardous negative protein trees in my brain, thank you very much. This also demonstrated the value of submission, because without confronting and hearing uncomfortable thoughts, I would not have realized what I needed to alter.

# Self-Control

I'm not a Stoic. I prefer the gentlest approach to almost anything. If I feel pressured, I wobble. But brace yourself, MDRC, for I'm about to quote a stoic at your pretty face!

'You have control over your thoughts, not external occurrences.

Recognize this and you will gain strength... Our lives are shaped by our thoughts.

— Marcus Aurelius

The term "self-control" kept coming to mind. I know it doesn't seem like a modern word or posture. Nor is it very hospitable to this delicate spirit.

Yes, my gut was correct; that was what I needed. Self-control became my watchword for this prize.

I had a flash of realization that our great baby-boomer (and even older) generation(s) would justifiably question our emphasis on emotional well-being, and that we should often buckle up and stop experiencing, digesting, and evaluating. That generation understands that there will be times when we must find the courage and control to persevere even when we believe we cannot. However, I believe we need both. We need the resilience to keep going, confident that we will not crumble in an improper manner. Nobody wants an inappropriate crumble! And we need to know that we have the right to collapse, unafraid of our ideas and feelings, when we can't be productive until they pass through us or we confront the problem.

At this point in my recovery, I needed to develop some discipline for what I was learning. I was still housebound, but the release of grief and expression of fury had given me a little more mental energy to concentrate. It was time for a gentle shove into self-control (not a 'button up and push on' moment), to implement some regular activities that would assist me in identifying any subconscious beliefs that may be influencing my physiology.

I thought about The Boy - or The Boy from Bristol, as I began to refer to him (because he was from Bristol; I know, I am so clever) - and how a love connection could be a distraction from my academics. The most essential relationship right now, I knew, was with myself as I continued to trek towards the new version of myself at the end of the cave I wanted to find. New but similar, I rediscovered the buried wild elements of my nineteen-year-old self that I missed and wanted.

I wondered. Might these gems be a love letter to that younger self?

## You Are A Lot Nicer Than You Think You Are!

The most difficult aspect of going under the hood at our thoughts is confronting and understanding our inner critic. We each have one. The internal critic is the bully who says things like, 'I can't believe you said that at the party; you're an idiot.' And this is her on a good day. The inner critic will be the one who tells you you aren't strong enough, funny enough, handsome enough, or successful enough - the one who has the meanest ideas and continuously tells you you need to improve in some manner.

When studying surrender, I discovered one of my favorite sayings: 'Rest is to be, without reporting on being.' We often unwittingly judge ourselves and report our failures: 'You didn't do that well enough, oh you made a mistake there, you're not as good as everyone else, you'll always fail in some manner, you shouldn't be crying, you should be over this illness by now.' ('Shoulds' usually means disgrace.) When we judge in this manner, I believe it is not too harsh to suggest that we are abusing ourselves internally. Under such a harsh rule, our wild selves are entirely worn down.

I'm happy to declare that there's no reason to berate ourselves for having an inner critic. It is one of the defensive mechanisms of childhood. Remember that we needed to belong to our caregiver in order to survive.

A friend told me she was on a date, and when she spontaneously burst out laughing, a thought from her past came to mind: Oops, that was too loud and stupid. She began regulating herself throughout the remainder of the meal, and her natural spark faded. A sense of guilt or shame can destroy a situation when, in reality, you are gorgeous and intelligent, and you can laugh as loudly and stupidly as you want.

The holy grail is to calmly observe the ideas, befriend and thank the inner critic for assisting us in survival, and rewire our brains to recognize that the thoughts are not our identities. It's incredible that we may quiet a harsh inner critic and begin to thrive without having to live under their dominion. Good word, FLOURISH.

Because, remember, MDRC, if we begin to live by core negative beliefs such as 'there's no use in me' or 'I'm not good enough,' that will be the mindset we work under. Our essential beliefs shape our entire lives, including our behaviour patterns, worries, and moods. MIND-BLOWING. If we believe we can't trust individuals, we may be afraid to form relationships and put up barriers. Anxious people begin to see danger everywhere, while angry people consider all the ways they have been harmed. If I had continued to believe that I would never recover, I would have curled up in my bed. Essentially, we constantly find proof for our beliefs.

Here's what you should believe, since it's true: you're a lot nicer than you realize. You are the perfect, one-of-a-kind, majestic elephant, and you deserve to be free of any thoughts that contradict this.

I'm pleased to be a broken record: there's only one of you. There has never been anyone like you, and no one will come after you. You are consequently truly remarkable and valued.

## Our Lovely Bodies

So here I was, MDRC, all fired up for some tangible instruments to effect change. But, focusing on the fact that there is only one of me, I was given the opportunity to confront another limiting idea head on. The classic 'I am not attractive' one. All of the tiny jibes from others or my inner critic had accumulated over the years to make me believe that being beautiful or sexy was unacceptable.

Another familiar feeling of sadness comes over me as I realize that even when I was gloriously young and lean (and could easily have been a beach babe extra on Home and Away), I was concerned and moaned about my body's appearance. I hear practically every lady over forty say the same thing. I mean, to be really honest with you, MDRC, I had a conventional supermodel shape in my youth and was frequently noticed as a catwalk model. I couldn't stroll along London's fashion district, King's Road, without being approached by a shop or brand. However, with this ridiculous concept in my brain unintentionally running the show, I would not inform anyone and throw away the cards. And when my body gained a significant amount of weight in my late twenties, I felt shame rather than self-compassion for having it as part of my life story.

Fortunately, I was able to change this limiting belief rather fast. All hail neuroplasticity! I simply began to accept the fact that no one else looked like me, and I gradually grew in love with my appearance and became friends with it. I developed a new route in my brain that strengthened my positive perception that I was attractive. There is just one of me, hence I am unique in beauty. Deal with it, world. I'm flourishing!

While getting to know The Boy from Bristol, I was able to be angry and weepy, but the prospect of being naked made me feel helpless. Despite the rewiring, an old kernel appeared (not a metaphor; we're in bad territory). After losing fitness owing to illness, I reverted to the old belief that I lacked sexy, womanly qualities. I wasn't sure if the loss of my perfect companion in Peggy would be replaced by another dog, a man, or both, but I knew there was more befriending of my physical appearance required. I didn't want to leave the love game because of fearful limiting ideas, especially since, I must admit, MDRC, I was getting increasingly captivated by The Boy from Bristol. I refocused on my true belief in the matter: that our bodies are an important part of us, but not the most important. Our bodies do not determine who we are.

More crucially, our body is a well tuned piece of sophisticated machinery that helps us live our lives and gives us life, but it is frequently chastised for failing to meet our expectations. We cannot return home to ourselves if we despise the body we have been given to live in. That is when a separation from our body can occur, making it easy to blank out, eat poorly, not recognize or accept how our bodies are feeling, become injured, and so on. We owe it to our health to befriend our beautiful bodies.

Oh, and acquire this heavy revvy; our bodies cannot lie. Examine your daily activities to determine what stresses your body and what relaxes and excites it. Our bodies deteriorate when we repeatedly make decisions based on fear, or 'shoulds' and 'musts'. All of the microbes in our daily lives have a direct impact on our physiology. MIND-BLOWING.

Our bodies are simply attempting to maintain equilibrium and heal themselves. They are completely efficient, bright, caring, and resourceful. I will be eternally grateful for having learned that our thoughts can come in the way of that process. When I became ill, I assumed that the problem was completely with my body. I was furious with it. It was time to work with it, challenge old beliefs, and continue to embrace and surrender to it in order to learn what it need to recover.

I recognized that the dream of having a quiet mind and being at ease inside myself was not a foolish, unattainable wish, but rather the path to good health.

# Laughter Really Is The Best Medicine

I wonder if the term 'laughing is the best medicine' is derived from the biblical aphorism 'a glad heart is good medicine'. On an experiential level, it feels true regardless of where it originated. Even a small laugh gives me a surge of energy and vitality. Now that we are so clever, MDRC, and understand that ideas are proteins that can be poisonous or the opposite, laughter is the biggest opposite and literally 'good medicine'. If you can approach your concerns lightly, the brain will no longer perceive them as a danger, allowing your system to settle and lessen tension and anxiety.

It can be an excellent tool in some situations. I have a friend with whom I refer to some recurrent ideas that have developed into anxieties as a 'serious threat'. They aren't, but our minds try to tell us they are (like the funnel-web spiders caught in cereal boxes in Sydney!), so my friend and I couldn't help but laugh at them by using comedy dramatic language, like a serious newsreader, of 'this is a serious threat'.

We may not utilize this on a particularly difficult top ten music in a gloomy patch, but we have tested with it. I'll never forget the first time we tested it out.

We opted to go canoeing with a two-person canoe. My friend was terrified of the idea of going in a canoe - the capsize risk, the physical strength required, and the fact that we were canoeing on a murky tidal river that she didn't want to fall into, especially since the tide could carry us downstream and out to sea (I know I have history here - this was years before my sinking mud experience!). I was already chuckling at her anxieties. Not unkindly, but we were already proving to ourselves how 'silly' our thoughts can be.

I began adding, 'The big threat is that we will have heat stroke and faint.' She laughed. She assumed I was joking. More evidence that my fainting concern was only a habit; it's not a genuine threat - as she pointed out, we don't frequently walk over the bodies of people who have fainted in the street! We were laughing at this point because she was concerned that if I fainted, she would lose control of the boat, causing us to capsize and be swept away. And then I was concerned that we would drink some of the water, which would undoubtedly cause terrible gastroenteritis! The amusement came from studying our many terrified thoughts, which the other couldn't grasp. Canoeing provides inadvertent therapy.

Finally, we set out. And everything was perfect. Although I was glad I wore a huge hat because the threat of sunstroke remained. My pal began warbling, 'Oh no, oh no, oh no,' which diverted me. No, this is a significant threat. I asked her what it was. The response was, 'That swan.' I struggled unsuccessfully to suppress my laughter. 'No, truly, this is a severe threat, seriously.' She warned me that if we entered the swans' waters, they might attack us, and they are strong enough to break a human's neck. I informed her that I believed it was an arm rather than a neck, but that it posed no real threat. If it were, there would be signs along the riverfront. People aren't continually fainting on the streets, and deathly swans don't attack humans every hour!

We giggled as she fearlessly swam upriver, passing the swan, who, of course, scarcely glanced our way.

After about an hour, it was getting really hot, so we decided to turn around with the tide so we wouldn't have to do so much paddling, head back, and get some shade. We made the reckless decision to take a shortcut back along a tributary.

We started paddling, and it became narrower, more overgrown, and more difficult to navigate. I was sweating in the hot noon sun and starting to feel worried. My friend was giggling at me. We had come across several eggs and broods, and there were approximately six really enormous swans approaching and surrounding us. I mean, even I felt threatened.

The only option was to turn around; we weren't going to make it through this tiny rivulet anyway. But try turning around a ten-foot canoe on a ten-foot-wide river while flanked by six irate hissing swans! We were in a state of complete terror and anxiety because we were under serious threat!!!

Of course, we made it out uninjured, with no swan death or fainting, and the canoe and our minds finally glided downstream as we concentrated on the beauty of the surroundings and the metaphor.

We demonstrate that our anxieties are simply habits, not universal truths. Dare to express your concerns (however stupid), I say.

# Loving Ourselves

## My Greatest Achievement

If you asked me, 'Miranda, what would you consider your greatest achievement?' I'd say, 'Thank you very much for asking such an exciting topic,' then pause thoughtfully and dramatically, possibly placing my palm on my chin and staring skyward like a true 'thinker'. Although it is a simple answer, I would use the pause for dramatic effect and to appear profound.

The response is that my greatest achievement has been learning to be kind and compassionate to myself, as well as rewiring my mind away from negative self-talk and judging.

In the past, I would have squirmed at these ideas. All I wanted to be was a strong, powerful, creative, enthusiastic, and productive woman. Now I understand that living strong is impossible without vulnerability. But I suppose that even five years ago, my greatest success would have been Miranda. It's definitely a close second.

I was developing a sitcom character whose only goal was to fall in love with herself. It was a narrative about how long it takes most women (and, I'm sure, many men) to stop trying to fit in and start loving and being themselves. I remember being perplexed when a female journalist labeled the show misogynistic. My Miranda character wore her heart on her sleeve, describing how difficult it was to be yourself in a world that told her she didn't fit in or have a place. I couldn't understand why another woman didn't identify with that idea or, at the very least, agree with how terrible it is that we should ever be made to feel 'bad' because of how we look, feel, or identify. I assumed that she must have been one of the lucky ones, that she must have always been pleased with her appearance and overall well-being.

But is there someone like that?! I sound bitter today, but I'm not, because it was a very beneficial reaction. It helped me clarify, while writing the show's ending, that I was going to bring my character together with the man she'd always wanted - but only if she didn't need him to justify herself. She had enough worth even without an attractive, easygoing man by her side to prove it. Are not we all? She needed to love herself in order to be free and well (and to love properly). Don't we all?

## Epiphany

I experienced an epiphany when the truth about loving oneself gradually permeated my mind and heart. All of the tough findings in the early, dark area of the cave pointed to this. This was the ultimate treasure. The one from which they would all hang. Without self-compassion and kindness, how could I allow myself to do the things I needed to do to heal? How could I communicate and beg for aid if I didn't first accept my situation? How could I continue my tale if I didn't compassionately let myself to feel and grieve? Without self-love, how can we begin to 'simply be ourselves'? How do we cease people-pleasing and putting on a mask to fit in if we lack self-esteem and the sense of belonging? Without understanding and loving oneself, how can we know which harmful thoughts to rewire away from and follow our own path? Without all of this, could I end up regretting not being true to myself?

As you know, I've been looking for basic watchwords for each treasure. If this treasure can be summed up in one word, it is kindness. Kindness is something we all need. It's another component of our fundamental identity. Remember, there is a purpose for you and your life! Everyone is important. According to Franciscan monk Richard Rohr, many people believe they are broken, sinful, and unlovable. Recognizing and accepting our fundamental nobility represents the ultimate paradigm change.

# Science Of Self-Care

It all started when I saw a woman on social media touting the benefits of self-care. I recall thinking, "Wait, that's not self-care; that's a privileged mini-break, isn't it?" It's more propaganda to make us feel inferior. It also promotes the myth that if we are hampered by sickness, poverty, burnout, or isolation, we will be unable to achieve self-compassion and esteem. I began my road to self-compassion with the smallest deeds from the confines of a bed. In your face, Norwegian chalet breaks!

This self-care nonsense appears to be ambiguous to me. That's fine, because it's preferable to being completely unaware of the situation. But it's too crucial to throw around. If someone who is struggling believes that self-care is only a treat, nothing changes, and we return to old habits, allowing unhelpful patterns to persist. We need to grasp the science of self-care.

I was frustrated because cultivating self-compassion was not something that came naturally for me. Another thing I wish had been on the school curriculum. Here I was, a decently intelligent (say nothing) middle-aged lady, suddenly confronted with the fact that she had practiced a strange and unknowingly modest amount of self-compassion throughout her life. I'd never been schooled about its importance or vitality, which was both humbling and furious. I had no choice but to understand a little more about the science.

Okay, MDRC, we can accomplish this. I'll direct you to my heaviest revvy as simply as I can. The first bit of research makes me sound strangely scholarly for a second, but don't worry. I'll fart soon, tell you what it sounds like, and everything will be back to normal. Please concentrate immediately!

So, get this: it can be difficult to promote self-compassion because we all have an ingrained, natural 'negativity bias'. Clever, eh? We are wired to belong, therefore we are naturally worried about our reputation and want to be valued by our community.

Our initial 'community', or relationship, is with our families. The safety of feeling recognized and understood, of being 'seen', is what helps us to build a healthy brain and neurological system while also developing a sense of self. As children, we need to know that our needs will be addressed because this is what teaches us to meet our own needs, which develops self-protection, expressiveness, and esteem. However, keep in mind that not every youngster will experience this sense of safety. The inner critic might then evolve.

So, get this. When we begin to assign negative worth to ourselves when it is unnecessary, criticism becomes damaging. Any criticism is viewed as a threat to the mind and body. This means that self-criticism might trigger a high-level terror reaction. Get this quote from Dr. Richard Davidson, noted for his pioneering studies on emotion and the brain:

Self-criticism can be detrimental to our mental and physical health. It can cause ruminative thoughts that reduce our productivity, as well as stimulate inflammatory pathways that lead to chronic sickness and premature aging.

I'm not happy that a long-term illness exposed me to the impacts of the inner critic (also known as a lack of self-compassion), but I'm glad I met her and was able to liberate myself from her. It's primarily about my situation, but I sincerely hope that it will be life-changing for you too.

Please bear with me as I try to explain it as best I can. Okay, here we go. Consider how the nervous system operates within a pot (or a jug - whatever container works best for you!). A stress pot. A pot that swings from calm at 1 to completely overwhelmed at 10. If we feel comfortable and tranquil, and life seems possible and manageable, our nervous system may be functioning on a 2 or 3 out of 10 scale. The stress pot is large; if faced with a challenging situation, such as an emergency at work, a health issue in the family, or a car breakdown in the middle of the road, the nervous system will respond with stress.

This fear response activates the limbic survival section of the brain, causing the heart to race, blood to flow to the muscles, and tunnel vision to provide the required singular focus to deal with the threat. This is a properly functioning neural system. MDRC, forgive me if you already know this, but what I've described above is the neurological system's natural flight-or-fight response. We are intended to be stressed. The neurological system is meant to fluctuate throughout the day for a variety of reasons, including performance anxiety, which might provide energy for a specific activity.

The thing I didn't realize - my life-changing revelation - was that our stress pots might become stuck on full. We may then continue to operate at a 9 out of 10, with no relief, eventually leading to a chronic stress response. Chronic stress, as opposed to a normal anxiety response, which fluctuates, means that one's system is constantly on high alert. Not so much fun, but I wouldn't be sharing if I hadn't discovered strategies to recover and reduce our stress levels to bearable levels. If you like, you can dig in with me.

Simply put, persistent stress impairs our physical and emotional well-being. The brain believes we are constantly under attack, so it has no time for joy, play, or optimism. If this condition persists for an extended period of time, we may develop secondary disorders such as discomfort, arthritis, skin problems, food sensitivities, or IBS. Stay with me if you can relate to any of this, because there is light at the end of the tunnel. I promise.

We can become chronically stressed for a variety of reasons, including a combination of a lack of sufficient sleep and food combined with overwork, which causes burnout.

My biggest stressor was physical stress from viral illnesses and injuries (the body experiences high levels of stress when fighting disease). Years of fear from misdiagnosed added to my stress level. Physical problems such as hypermobility and PoTS were added. My workload increased (even though I enjoyed and desired it). The simple fact of living in a bustling metropolis in a fast-paced environment was added. All the terrible patterns I had gotten into were added. Then there was the stress of stress. Will I make it through the day? Should I eat this or will it give me a migraine? Am I doing too much or not enough?

For years, I had woken up with symptoms that I now realize were caused by a stress pot at a 9 out of 10, as a result of my untreated Lyme and accompanying infections from an immune system problem. Anything I had to do that day would be extremely exhausting. This is why I eventually collapsed.

Get it. Have you ever noticed how you can feel down, tired, and even anxious when you have a cold or flu? That's because the immune system responds appropriately to eliminate the invader. The immune system is related to the neurological system, and both are heightened. After getting the message from our brain, the immune system cleverly gives us symptoms to send us to bed while ensuring that we do what is necessary to rid ourselves of the illness.

The symptoms are not caused by the sickness, but by our brain. MIND-BLOWING. Cue signs of anxiousness, a feeling of being wired, or difficulty sleeping, along with foggy exhaustion. When the cold virus is eliminated, the brain switches off its fight, flight, or freeze alert reaction; the threat has passed. Our bodies are performing exactly what they were supposed to accomplish.

If we contract a virus or infection while our immune system is dysregulated, it is unable to eliminate it. It is already working overtime, so it exclaims, 'Help, we don't have enough resources to remove this illness; throw more at it.' The neurological and immunological systems then activate more, resulting in inflammation and even more severe symptoms than usual.

So, drumroll, GET THIS: research now suggests that this is how long-term diseases like long Covid and ME/chronic fatigue syndrome (CFS) begin. Basically, once the acute virus has left the body, the immune system never receives the message. It continues to release adrenaline into the body to combat the sickness. The weariness persists, other latent infections awaken, and secondary issues and symptoms develop while the brain remains on high alert. That summarizes the condition. When ME first became common in the 1980s, it was dubbed 'yuppie flu'. This makes sense to me now. High-functioning, highly wired, fast-paced city workers and others were getting it because their stress levels were at a ten out of ten simply by living. (Of course, this is not limited to city workers.) One virus would be sufficient to induce the disease because the body was unable to eliminate it. There are many university students burning the candle at both ends, athletes pushing their bodies to the maximum, and mothers working long hours. For others, it's the unaware accumulation of tension - which is why I'm so concerned about disrupting unhelpful worldly behaviors, as it became evident they generate stress.

Yes, it was true: my nervous and immunological systems would not be able to return to balance unless my stress reaction was lowered. Until this happened, my body was unable to rid the Lyme and other diseases that were destroying me. I finally understood why getting out of bed had become impossible for my lovely body.

It is critically vital to emphasize that this is a physical issue.

So, MDRC, if you can, join me in my excitement despite the circumstances. This was the most significant insight since I now understand that my brain is changeable. I may use my thinking to signal to my brain that the threat has passed, allowing my immune system to resume normal function. EXTRAORDINARY.

Suddenly, all of the treasures were glowing lights that made scientific, diagnostic sense: minimize stress, meet your needs, look after yourself, and relieve yourself of the obligation to continuously 'be better'. Love yourself. Not because it sounds wonderful, but because it promotes good health. I felt as if I had finally received some type of guidebook. I had means to reintegrate myself into the world in an authentic and tranquil manner, allowing me to function effectively rather than striving to keep up with the world's pace.

We're told that no matter how hard we work, our best isn't good enough. We must learn to comfort ourselves. Or, as the 'ists' put it, to'reparent ourselves'. This certainly made sense given what I was learning in this treasure.

If the science of self-care is ultimately about meeting our vital needs in order to reduce an overburdened stress pot, then when we intentionally have a bubble bath and a take-away pizza because, for example, we said no to something we knew we didn't have capacity for and thus stopped ourselves from people-pleasing to prove we are loved, we are rewiring old patterns. The act transforms us, resulting in actual self-care.

# The Beautiful Bluebell Bulb

Even after researching into and accepting the clear science (and hearing of thousands of people cured of similar diseases to mine), a part of me from the past would occasionally arise and wonder whether 'loving oneself' was indeed the ultimate answer, and the place to begin. It's tempting to believe that the minor actions we take every day are meaningless or won't result in any bodily change. My interest was piqued, and my understanding was securely anchored in an exciting way. It was through a gorgeous wooden crate of bluebell bulbs.

I'd been locked inside again due to a flare-up of viral symptoms (shingles this time - hello, gorgeous 'temporary tattoos'!), and a buddy kindly brought some nature to brighten up my literal and metaphorical insides. The bulbs were sitting high in the earth, with a few green shoots growing from each.

I was reminded of a plant experiment conducted in a classroom for youngsters. The teacher had read of a fascinating 'rice experiment' in which a professor, Dr Masaru Emoto, placed two bowls of the identical cooked rice in a fridge and murmured love words over one and horrible, toxic words over the other. The bowl that had been badly spoken over began to mould in a way that the other had not. I know! Discuss the power of words. The teacher gave the students plants to look after for their version of the experiment.

I decided to try my own experiment. I glanced at my gorgeous bluebell bulbs, chose one in the corner, stroked it, and began speaking in the same tone that my inner critic had used to describe my condition that day. Things like 'it's your responsibility', 'you let yourself down yesterday', and 'you'll never be well'. An unexpected thing happened: projecting those comments onto an innocent living thing was more heartbreakingly awful than I could have predicted. I couldn't keep on; it felt awful to be so cruel even to a bluebell bulb.

If it hurts to injure someone else, it hurts to hurt oneself. In that instant, I knew I would never entertain my inner critic again. It was at least half as large as the rest. The others stood tall, proud, and robust, flanked by three or four smaller offshoots. The one I was cruel to was shorter, with no offshoots. Watching this happen in front of my eyes, rather than merely on paper as part of a scientific project, changed me forever.

I was also struck - and this upset me - by how easy it had become, after that guilt-inducing first day, to 'abuse' that bluebell bulb. I'd fast gotten desensitized. I assumed this was because I was used to having these negative views about myself. From now on, I was going to do everything I could to fill my life with self-compassion and kindness.

We are not who our inner critics believe we are.

# Pipe Down, Sandy!

Before we continue, here's a humorous but smart approach to remove an inner critic that may be influencing you that I learned from Martha Beck, Kristin Neff, and Steven Hayes (all the 'ists' would agree). They recommend naming and picturing one's inner critic (which we all have to varied degrees). This may sound like more, rather than less, crazy, but I found it to be a powerful act. If you dare to learn about your top ten thinking tunes and a critic's personality, my recommendation is to lean in. Our critics will be all different.

Without further ado, I'd like to present you to my Sergeant Major Sandy! She's dressed in a safari suit, with broad khaki shorts to the knees and long white socks pulled up. Of course, you'll need a hardhat. She's the one that gets freaked out when we're late, wants everything done right away, despises anything left on a to-do list, and doesn't want to spend any time. I don't mind that about her. Sandy will be checking Google Maps to ensure we don't sit in traffic unnecessarily (we normally leave an extra half an hour early anyway), she will never miss an aircraft, and she always keeps an emergency energy bar in her bag. We all need Sandy to some level (each of us has a planning and organizing aspect of our brain). The trouble is when she goes into sergeant major mode and paces around, puts on her hard hat, and pulls out a whip! Then she tells me I'm lazy and that I should get up at five a.m., as she's seen people on Instagram say is the best way to maximize the day.

Naming and imagining her proved to be really effective. I could laugh at her. I could celebrate what I enjoyed about her, and then begin to say, 'Oh, do pipe down, Sandy,' when it was an attack that didn't serve me or that I knew would put strain on my body. I was in power because I had dragged her out of her unconsciousness. It was not lunacy, but genius from the 'ists'. It was the epitome of kindness.

Doing this work is profound. It's like escaping from prison. I knew the revelatory diagnosis that my body was in a chronic stress response was correct because anytime I instructed Sandy to shut up, I noticed a difference in my body. Similarly, when I submitted and felt or expressed emotion, the tension was released. My stress level was being decreased.

It was fundamentally about self-compassion.

# Don't Go Breaking My Heart

I wondered whether this basic value about loving ourselves was preparing me for a love relationship. I was thinking about The Boy from Bristol more and more. In between sofa chats, we spent a lot of time FaceTiming. He complimented me one evening on my appearance. I said, 'Thank you.' It seemed unexpectedly unfamiliar, but forceful and 'correct'. Not only because I FaceTimed with the camera in favorable dim lighting. One step at a time.

Whether I was preparing for a relationship or not, I knew I had to just let it happen (see my surrender). The route to self-compassion begins with accepting that we are enough on our own. We cannot derive our worth from outside of ourselves. I'd taken both of those realities to heart, and I was not going to fall into the trap of viewing a love partner as a savior. No, sir!

My thoughts evolved further (I considered myself quite the philosopher by this point). MDRC, I wondered: can you truly love if you're wearing a mask of any sort? Surely genuine love entails the ability to exhibit and be revealed the truth of who we are, without shame or judgment? If I liked myself, I could remove the masks and be completely honest about who I was. This meant that I could be loved and loved more. That remained my purpose, whether The Boy from Bristol ended up being my person or someone placed in my path to learn from.

The following time we FaceTimed, I was given another chance to be completely myself. We were about to end the call when he inquired what I was going to do with the remainder of my evening. I responded, 'I'm going to do some Lego.' A little pause. He said, 'Sorry, did you say you were going to play Lego?!' I proceeded confidently. Yes, I did. 'Do they have names?' he inquired. 'No,' I said in all my seductive magnificence, 'I name them myself.' As I hit the pillow that night, I had to order Sandy to stop talking!

In her book The Way of Integrity, Martha Beck describes a research that demonstrated that telling just three fewer white lies each week lowered unpleasant feelings and health concerns. I find that completely fascinating. I know it would have destroyed my heart and weakened me if I had lied to The Boy from Bristol. Everything was telling me to stay on track and release my wild, genuine self.

Have we become so linked with our inner critic or the outside world that we have lost who we are? Perhaps the act of attempting to keep up with the world is enough to cause chronic stress in the nervous and immune systems.

It was time to look at the patterns that made loving myself so difficult, or not a natural part of my existence. Uncovering any harmful or unhelpful patterns would provide practical methods to love myself, not to mention the hope I felt for the physiological shift this could bring. I was revved up with my strong revvy.

# Pleasing The Peoples Or Codependency – Now What?!

I was still reeling from needing, when I was confronted with the concept of codependency. Pia Mellody, an expert 'ist' in this field, defines codependency as the persistent neglect of oneself in order to seek praise, love, or validation from another else. Ouch, how heartbreaking.

The complete opposite of liking oneself. Most of which I felt quite fortunate not to live beneath.

MDRC, it's such a waste of time to worry about what others might think of us. We never know what others will think of us. As Mel Robbins recently stated on her show, "You will never, ever live the life you are meant to live if you are constantly concerned about what other people are thinking." People can have different perspectives about you while still loving you.

For example, should we avoid saying, 'What do you want, anything you want, I don't mind, well you go first, no after you …'? It's exhausting! People-pleasing suggests that instead of expressing your wants, you should conform to the norm. However, as I already stated, clarity is kindness, and we must continue to free ourselves by expressing our preferences and dislikes.

I become moderately upset when I ask, 'Shall we eat?' and the response is, 'I don't mind, maybe I could eat.' And I think, "Well, I know you can eat." I've seen you, and you're extremely adept at eating; you know how to use a knife and fork. I know you could eat, but would you want to? It's so beautiful when someone excitedly exclaims, 'I would really like to eat,' or firmly says, 'Thanks, but I'm not hungry.' We're having an enormously better time.

If I sound cocky since I don't suffer from this often crippling feature, don't worry, I was quickly corrected. As a result, many independent and 'successful' individuals do not exhibit codependency. Now what?! So I've been codependent? RUDE!

But I am happy since her idea confirmed for me, once and for all, that such behaviors, while frequently acclaimed, are plainly not kind or loving to oneself and would significantly contribute to the stress pot. Fortunately, with Treasure One firmly in my pocket, I was gradually stepping out of those habits.

# What Are Boundaries? And Now What?!

Another buzzword is 'boundaries'. But how many of us actually understand what it means? I did not. More studying for me.

Boundaries define our obvious lines and limits. Our physical and emotional defenses against others. Without them, it is difficult to love and defend ourselves, which can lead to low energy. When we have strong and healthy boundaries, we accept responsibility for our own thoughts, feelings, and conduct while keeping them distinct from those of others.

Boundaries promote healthy ways of life by encouraging us to care for ourselves, respect ourselves so that we are treated as equals, feel safe to express our emotions, be okay with conflicts, and know who we are and what we like.

Everything sounded fantastic in theory.

But hang on un petit momento (a lovely little French-Italian combination there …) - here was all the complexity and intricacies of humanness. To go forward with self-love, I had to accept some vulnerability and ask for help, which probably made me a babbling, crying mess at times. But I also had to be forceful in establishing my clear and exact boundaries, and with my head held high, say what I required, nay demanded! To a person I know. And at the risk of people not understanding, being upset with me, or believing I was impolite. EVEN THE CONCEPT! Furthermore, the 'ists' informed me that being misunderstood would be an inevitable part of the process. FOR GOODNESS' SAKE, WHAT NOW?!

It helped me grasp the nuances of limits even more when I saw how amusingly scary it was to begin creating them. Being housebound was not the easiest option, but possibilities arose. This was the first one.

The pause continued, but the new boundaried me was resolved not to give up. I couldn't not fill the gap, so I explained, 'I know it's difficult to comprehend, but I truly need a calm night to myself...'

She gazed again, as if I had ordered her to toss a small kitten into a river. (Sorry!)

And then she answered, "No, of course, nice idea; I'll probably ask my husband anyway." Wow, have a wonderful evening. That is just wonderful of you. Amazing.' She acted as if I had just won the Nobel Peace Prize. I could tell that had gotten her thinking: are we really allowed to speak what we need?

Yes we are! And that was another important step in regaining energy and feeling more like myself. A lack of boundaries can greatly increase stress levels.

It was a relief to hear that setting boundaries with others to protect ourselves and our energy does not imply that you do not love them. In fact, it's the opposite. People in healthy, safe relationships respect each other's empowering and resourcing limits. It could be the key to loving more.

# Why We Do What We Do

## Off To Work We Go

My house had been a safe haven throughout my illness. I created various 'zones' to 'do' disease as best I could. There was a cozy armchair that overlooked the small garden, where you could watch the birds. I then sipped from my favorite tea mug while attentively savouring some dipped dark chocolate. It was also a relaxing spot to practice breathing techniques (when I had the discipline to do so). There was a Lego table near the flames. And I set up a 'day nap and exercise space' where I could stretch or do light tai chi motions. I was dealing with illness as best I could; I failed in some manner every day, but that was fine. I was gradually reducing tension in my pot.

All of this contributed to my newfound sashaying vitality, which prompted me to question my place outside of a sickbed. I wondered if it was time to set up a work zone. I felt a flutter of joy at the prospect of getting back to some work. Was it time to write a fresh comedic script? A few producers had inquired whether I would adapt any works into movies. I'd had to politely decline, but perhaps I was ready to saunter into my email inbox and announce that I was now willing to discuss it. Plus, how lovely it would be to have a worthwhile distraction.

I had missed work so much. And I liked the thought of returning with a healthy, well-rounded mindset based on what I had learned, and continued to learn, about how I uniquely tick. Was it time? As if to convey to my head that it was, I did a short march and a skip to go to work, humming the Disney classic: 'Heigh-Ho…'.

# Get Out Of Your Home But Stay In Your Home

A global pandemic is not what a lady who has begun to sashay and skip after many years of considering returning to work needs. Does anyone? At any time?

It was an odd point in my story because I'd been advised, based on the remaining cluster of symptoms I still had, including some residual fatigue (which meant, frustratingly, that some aspects of my work were still impossible), to consider mould poisoning as one of the reasons my immune system might still be malfunctioning. Mould poisoning?! I had never heard of such a thing.

I was certain this couldn't be the case, but my body's inflammation levels were high enough to merit research. I was waiting for the results of a 'dust swab' on my residence, which involves analyzing dust to determine air quality and toxin levels. I was advised to leave if the dust swabs returned highly hazardous results. This was happening at the same time as Covid news was making its way over our airwaves, and the threat of 'lockdown' loomed. If that became a reality, it would be criminal to not be in your own house.

And then the results arrived. On both fronts. Mold toxicity levels in my residence were ten times the World Health Organization's permissible level. I was told to leave as soon as possible with only clothes and basics, but due to lockdown in two days, I was forced to stay at home. I was shocked.

My own home, which had become my shelter, was contributing to my illness, and I needed to leave as soon as possible before it became illegal to do so. I spent a very nervous day browsing rental websites, unsure where to go and how to make it work. Until, happily, I remembered a friend who was away, couldn't return, and might let me remain in her home. She did. Thank God for kindness.

With the gift of a roof over my head, I found the first lockdown to be a happy couple of months. I recall feeling horrible about it as I witnessed the carnage around me. But I know that most people who are housebound due to an ailment that reduces their vitality will tell you that they had the same joy.

For the first time, we felt a release from the everyday agony of disappointment in all we wished to be able to achieve, things that (healthy) others may take for granted. We weren't alone in our disappointment. People were more willing to communicate and FaceTime. We were literally not alone either.

What astonished me, MDRC, was how relieved I was that most work was not a possibility. Odd, given how pleased I had been to get back to it. But it made me realize how much stress I'd been under from missing my job for so long. I was always analyzing whether my body was strong enough to go back, even when it wasn't. It was work that I pushed myself to complete before collapsing and giving up. It was especially sad that I had to stop working so soon after my first appearance in a Hollywood film (Spy). There was also a game show remake in the United Kingdom. Exciting potential that, in the end, I never got to explore. I was gutted, to say the least.

It was a wonderful lift. For a time. And then, in the spirit of being honest with myself, I discovered, rather ashamed at first, that the most difficult aspect of my life to let go of had been employment. Did I place a higher priority on work than on other, more important, things? Was it via employment that I gained significance and worth? We frequently establish our identities through it; we all require a job or function; growing and perfecting our talents is part of what allows us to thrive; we all need to pay our expenses; and we may even feel lost without work because it is such an important identify. But if I were to return with a healthy attitude, it couldn't be the only thing that characterized me.

My job is unique in the sense that you 'get noticed' in a manner that other jobs do not. The job is simply to be observed and stared at! One woman with chronic exhaustion was a teacher who described feeling as if she was clutching on by her fingernails to avoid having to retire. A large part of her felt lost without her identity as a teacher.

This appears to be yet another conditioned response. The belief that labor has not just a very high (and frequently skewed) value, but that we might sometimes feel as if we only truly exist, or exist at our finest, when we have a job. Without realizing it, work had become the most important element of my life, and its loss was severely felt. It was difficult to feel complete without, well, hard work. I have to acknowledge that I felt less without it. I was ready to heigh and ho, off to work, but first I needed to discover more about my distinct identity and how I ticked. To ensure that it was not job that made me feel whole as a person. This became the next treasure to lean on.

I knew God could operate in mysterious ways, but - get this, MDRC - I discovered that the lyrics to the Disney song I had been humming were about - wait for it - coming home from work. I didn't have a physical house to call my own, which made the soul-searching even more intense. I had no choice but to continue searching for that home within myself and who I was, without the external identifying me.

Finding out who I was outside of work was a true blessing.

# The Wild

As you may have guessed, when I did gain strength and was able to take short journeys, I gravitated toward nature. So, a couple of years after the mould and Covid catastrophe, I returned to the Knepp Estate and its incredible rewilding initiative to reflect on this work. To survive, people must be in the present moment. They will perish if they sit around worrying or contemplating. If they don't trust their intuition, they die. We are loved without any proof, simply by existing. Have we forgotten that our identity is not defined by our work? Even if we lose our employment (which many of us will for a variety of reasons), we remain the most vital aspect of our magnificent self.

I had no idea how much I had lost sight of that until a time at Knepp. I was enjoying a modest walk, thrilled to be moving with a little more freedom, delighted to be in fresh air, and completely absorbed in the moment by the nature, when someone yelled upon recognizing me. That was fine; she was initially complimentary, and I cracked a corny joke about being her best wildlife sight of the day: 'The Miranda Beast'. She didn't really understand, which was awkward, but there was no time for a cringing quiet when she asked me, 'Have you retired, then?' My ego performed a big cartwheel.

I amusedly defensive to this poor, innocent woman: 'Um, no, I have not retired, thank you very much to you, just taken some time, had some stuff going on, and then there's been Covid, hasn't there, so you know … Retired? No, I am here; look, hello. And my show is still on iPlayer, I'm here, hello, I'm relevant, and so on. (I was about to look up my CV online and recite a monologue.) We all have an ego to some extent, but my reaction was strong enough to make me examine whether my identity had become, at least in part, entwined with work.

Good day, MDRC. I just looked up from my laptop (I'm writing this piece from Knepp, again) and was met with an astonishing sight of nature in this wood. I'm in a congested, human-infested area of Southern England and may have been rammed by a stag and pecked by a kestrel.

But what amazing wildness to see. I want to be that free and at ease with myself, without a certain function or job to define me, feeling majestic despite the fact that others assume I've retired! To just be. Is that actually possible? Not pursuing a profession or feeling pressure to 'move ahead'. Not dreading the outcome, but simply working as part of being. Couldn't I just be like that stag, wandering through the woods and occasionally killing or rutting something?

When did work become about prestige and importance? Shouldn't it be about the 'why'? Why are the values dependent on more than one notch on the CV? The red stag didn't need a LinkedIn page to establish himself. Certainly, thinking of dolloping some goodies on my patch (sounds weird) while I was healing made illness-related seclusion much easier. It began to dispel any lingering feelings of insignificance. Just scatter crumbs of goodness around, I reasoned!

When I discovered author, researcher, and speaker Simon Sinek's work on 'Finding a Why', it became the foundation of this gem. That was what this time would be about. Finding my why. According to Simon Sinek, having a why and purpose statement is important for both businesses and individuals. That would wake me up in the morning if I worked for Spotify (though I understand that most firms have challenges we don't always like). Astriid, a nonprofit I discovered during lockdown, has a lovely mission statement: 'Helping people with long-term health challenges and their carers find meaningful employment so that the routine and sense of normality can provide a stronger sense of well-being.' Simon Sinek's personal why is 'to inspire people to pursue the things that motivate them, so that, together, each of us may change our world for the better'. Our why is about who we are rather than what we do; it serves as a filter for everything from volunteering to the types of movies he enjoys watching. He gets stirred up when others are motivated. Simon claims that once he discovered his specific why, he stopped talking about what he did and instead talked about what he believed. He stated that starting with a why revolutionized his life and allowed him to live it with meaning. Yes, please. I am in.

If you want to hone your why, MDRC (Simon, for example, offers an online course). And you're never forced to share it with another human if you don't want to. Given that I have already shared so much with you in this book, I will tell you how mine began. Writing the book helped clarify its purpose.

To let people recognize themselves outside the world's laws and demands, as well as their own pasts. To allow people to be who they are meant to be, so that the world is healthier and happier.

It sounds quite grand (I'm cringing a little!). But I have to say that it quickly made my life feel more fascinating and gratifying, regardless of the job, discussions, or small ways I choose to use it. Yes, I'm all in. I'm going to prance around like a crazy stag.

# The Success Trap

Many people fall into a success trap because they want - or need - to show themselves through their work. It is not in a nice or caring manner.

I do not believe that success is a terrible thing. Sometimes it's just a byproduct of doing what we enjoy. The pitfall is believing that achievement defines who we are and can serve as a foundation for happiness. A 'why' refers to something other than achievement and measurement. Think about it, MDRC. If a person's why is to get popularity, they will always be afraid of losing it; if a person's why is 'to be the best', they will always be under enormous competitive pressure and will compare themselves to others.

Rutger Bregman's book Humankind was an intriguing read for me. He made an interesting point when he stated that we have grown increasingly concerned with ourselves and our own personal benefit. Our focus has shifted away from friendship, community, and spirituality and toward the trap of accomplishment. But - and this is a game changer - our goals can never be effective unless they are motivated by a desire to make a difference.

I was encouraged, MDRC. I reflected on how well this relates to learning to love oneself as a never-selfish act. For when we begin to understand ourselves in this way (with our whys), we may discover that we have an impact on the community around us. Dollop our goodies all over the place!

But that is enough about doing good for the larger world. Return to me! I was in a really odd situation; it's not often that you find yourself that far apart from the rest of the world. I was able to continue to stand back and witness what the rat race was doing to my loved ones, and it all seemed insane. Frenzied. I became nervous when friends informed me about their professional lives.

Many people did not appear to enjoy or be enthusiastic about their work. The demand to be continually available had certainly gotten worse. I would hear comments like, 'I'm exhausted, but I should go to this event so that I may be seen as a team player.' A constant sensation of needing to prove and keep up. All the carrying on, in all its messiness. I worried about my friends. I wasn't seeing folks skip to work or skip back; instead, they were limping home.

I determined that the only way to make work a healthy, functioning part of ourselves was to figure out why we do what we do. Which, ironically, makes it lot easier to knock on doors, go to job interviews, and start the first day of a job, because it's not just about our evaluation, how we move ahead, and so on; it's also about how we bring some good into that workplace. When I was in my twenties data inputting at an office, it didn't particularly excite me, but looking back, I saw that I was acting on my 'why' outside of work, with suggestions for fun during lunch breaks or hosting things after we clocked out.

I recall Treasure One's teachings on gathering and how hosting is an excellent way to fulfill our individual 'whys'. I sincerely hope that if I ever return to data entry, I will be able to reframe it. Instead of focusing on how I perceived it (as a tedious task), I would be able to understand how it was assisting others in becoming freed, because the firm required that efficiency to function well. Stamp your 'why' on the ordinary, and those duties may become more interesting and fulfilling.

I remember conversing with the project manager in charge of my house's remodeling, the man who de-molded me (stable). I questioned why he had taken on the assignment, given that the mould was unusual and thus complicated. He responded, "After hearing about your health problems and knowing the building industry, I felt compelled to do my best for you and protect you." Talk about a serving of goodness.

## You Can Do Anything You Set Your Mind To'

I know this is an often used slogan that inspires many individuals. However, as guidance, it has never been particularly effective for me. It's always felt like a pressure to me. So, when I read these words from clinical neurologist Dr Caroline Leaf: 'You can achieve what you are predisposed to do with your genes and your skills', I felt instantly calmer and more encouraged.

It felt a lot gentler, too. The way to love ourselves is to discover and develop our unique skills and gifts. Going our own path, against worldly expectations and patterns, with our unique set of skills that the world requires and desires, is bold and courageous. I think. And hopefully, considerably more satisfying.

It makes perfect sense for each person to have a unique DNA and set of gifts. Each exists solely on this planet at this point in history. You may be the next great artist, politician, salesperson, inventor, train driver, human resources manager, nurse, farmhand, babysitter, writer, gardener, explorer, fundraiser, parent, administrative assistant, shopkeeper, or zoo manager. Everything you do matters. We're all unique, strange wonders with a point!

# Remember What You Love

Remembering what you love may seem like a simple concept, but it's a clever method to find what's missing from your life. Thinking on what thrills you and your innate passions unlocks the stressful and striving brain, allowing you to rediscover the genuine you, rather than the one who has worn a mask for years. Not the 'you' shaped by past training.

All of the 'isms' I read on finding our why emphasized that we needed to free our imaginations in order to get back to the basics of what we just enjoyed doing. It doesn't matter whether it makes no sense, sounds immature, or has nothing to do with a work; we can simply allow our thoughts to wonder. Dots can be linked later.

I like that remark since the prosperity trap frequently causes us to lose that emotion. Many may have never felt it. Which is why I think it's fantastic because remembering what you love eventually leads to dreaming.

When I was really ill, someone asked me, 'What would you do if your symptoms and condition simply disappeared?' At the moment, I couldn't imagine or respond to that. I realized I needed to dream again.

I've subsequently discovered that by dreaming about the things that bring us joy, purpose, and excitement, we are telling the brain that we are not afraid, reminding it of potential, which lessens the stress response and strengthens the immune system. You might as well dream!

Considering my why provided views into the 'new me' who could now be free of any former success traps, allowing me to feel meaningful whether I stayed, became ill, or ended up back on a film set.

A dream job is not what we are looking for (some may never achieve their precise work goals), but rather a why inside our skills that is a reflection of who we are. And dream big about it.

I will never stop dreaming and pursuing what I enjoy and what thrills me. And I'm sorry my younger self was partially locked in the arrivals hall because she thought she had to.

## Time To Tap In

A little later, I was watching an acting class. One activity had the group stand on the outside around two players in the center, and it was up to those on the outside to 'tap in' when they felt inspired to play, exchanging with whoever they tapped out. Following the exercise, the teacher provided feedback and asked the few students who had never participated why they felt they hadn't. There was no admonishment because they were under no responsibility to do so.

They admitted to being caught up in the watching, and the teacher gently pushed them to listen deeper, privately, to see if there was any fear-based reason they preferred watching. Because, as she astutely pointed out, we might fall into fear-based patterns without even realizing it.

We do need to 'tap in'. Dreams are not only for other people. Everyone can have a unique calling because they are unique! It's not limited to certain types of people. And some of the greatest changemakers emerged from little. Where we begin is not a barrier to how we will end.

There is nothing to lose by joining in.

'What if you wake up someday at 65 or 75 and you never wrote your memoir or novel, or you didn't go swimming in those warm pools and oceans all those years because your thighs were jiggly and you had a nice big comfortable tummy, or you were just so strung out on perfectionism and people-pleasing that you forgot to have a big juicy creative life, of imagination and radical silliness and staring off into space like a kid? It is going to break your heart. Do not let this happen. — Anne Lamott

# Play

## 'It's Time To Get Your Joy Back'

I remember waking up one morning and shouting out loud, 'Right, Miranda, it's time to get your joy back; it's time to follow joy.' It was a small, odd moment.

I knew this was a defining moment. I didn't feel like I had lost all joy, and I wasn't depressed. So, where did this powerful, definite voice telling me it was time to reclaim my joy originate from? A scuttling noise in the corner of the room interrupted my thought process. I suspected it was a mouse, and I was not in the mood to deal with one. (Are we ever? It's difficult to find delight in vermin. But when I dared to approach the strange noise, I noticed a big butterfly flapping against an unopened window.

What a gorgeous creature. Its orange and white markings are exquisitely detailed, as are the fragility and strength of its wings. The same thing happened as always when I observe an animal in distress: I became distressed. This time, there was no panic; I simply looked at it and murmured, 'Oh, poor thing, you seem absolutely bored and worn.' Exhausted from the struggle to escape into its native habitat, which it could see plainly but was blocked by an impenetrable glass jail; bored because it was in a room it was not meant to be in.

It was created to decorate, out there in the world, beneath the vast sky. How sensible, I thought. Don't rush to celebrate your liberation; instead, stay there for now, gather your strength, let your unpleasant experience wash over you, and leave when you're ready. There is no rush, my beautiful butterfly. This, for the astute among you, was clearly poised to become another metaphor! I was more concerned than usual for this wonderful creature since, on this particular day, I, too, was fatigued and bored. I felt trapped and wanted to flee. This must be why I awoke and said, 'It's time to follow joy.'

I've heard that cyclists train not to avoid potholes, but to see the way between them. If the exercise was 'don't look at the potholes,' their brain would focus on them, feel afraid, and inadvertently drive into them. Instead, they practice to look for a clear passage between the holes.

Looking back - and this is why my campfire moment was so crucial to me - I can see that I'd grown bored and fatigued from years of focusing on the potholes, conquering them, mitigating against them, and attempting to control them. I've said potholes so many times that it no longer seems like a word, and it's become somewhat impolite. POTHOLES!

When we were younger, playfulness and delight were normal parts of our day. We don't dwell on life's pitfalls because we're always looking for the next idea that will provide us with energy, creativity, and enjoyment. And we automatically, physically and symbolically, hop to it.

Yes, it's partly because we have younger bodies and less responsibility, but I believe all tired adults have found solace in moments of play. I had reached a healing plateau, and that voice I heard when I awoke was most likely the cause. If we consistently regard life as a series of challenges to overcome, we cannot help but grow fatigued.

I was living in a limited way, internally flapping and agitated, like a butterfly confined in the room. I could see life and all I cherished beyond the glass. I was a wild beast who had unintentionally snookered herself. Even I, a goofy creative who despised rules and talked about freeing people free, had been beaten down. Not just because of my recent illness, but because I had fallen into yet another worldly trap: play was unimportant. This was a stunning epiphany, and it made me realize how much fun had been sucked out of my life. Joy, I hoped, would be another gem on my journey back to my wild side. Another gem for mending.

I was fairly confident of what joy was.

That is the first thing I learned about joy. It's all about the small moments. Little moments of joy undermine the ego and thinking mind that may be envious of someone who owns a superyacht, because surely having a personal chef to give constant canapés while lounging on a front deck is joy?

I know deep down that those are examples of fleeting happiness, if we ever experience anything slightly similar. (For me, it would probably be a takeaway because I pretend the delivery came from my personal chef.) Otherwise, all wealthy individuals would tell us that the 'answer to life' is their lifestyle, and where would that leave the world's poor? No, that makes absolutely no sense.

Joy must be about astonishment. It's all about plants, clouds, smiles, and hot tea. And butterflies. It's about ordinary things. Not the accolades, examination results, promotions, or bank balance. All of these things are transient and finite. Joy says, 'Sorry, I couldn't care less if you were employee of the month; LOOK AT THAT PETAL IN THE RAIN, ISN'T IT AMAZING?!'

The thing about joy is that there will always be something like a petal in the rain to discover in every moment. That is what joy feels like to me: grace. I suddenly missed Peggy's velvety fur; caressing a pet is a great example of delight and comfort.

The grace of joyful moments doesn't always feel as resonant without someone to share it with, and joy is always a deep connector, but there are times when we are alone, and it's worth considering that joy is just a reason for being. It nourishes our souls. It's another aspect of who we are. That indicates that my thoughts and dreams are what bring me delight. This is where I create. Laugh. Experience the wonders of nature. Feel like you belong (I discovered that my developing faith provided me with an unexpected sense of connectivity and joy).

It's undoubtedly an important component of our identity. I read that even in the depths of grief, joy provides a break for our nervous systems. It provides us with natural neurotransmitters and substances to help our fatigued brains recover and keep the negative bias at bay. Healthy neurotransmitters are essential for maintaining a healthy brain, which leads to proper immunological and nervous system function.

We require oxytocin, dopamine, serotonin, and endorphins to survive and thrive, and they are produced while we play. This is why children gravitate to it. Science, quite excitingly, continued to measure the treasures. Following delight is crucial for regaining a healthy body.

It was time to burn off the leftover ennui and tiredness. To finally train my thoughts away from the potholes and rediscover play, which was undoubtedly the portal to a lot more delight. I told you the riches become more cheerful!

# Forgetting To Play

When asked if there was a specific time when I realized I wanted to pursue a career in comedy, I have a clear answer. I'll never forget it. This is remarkable because I have a terrible memory (Lyme-type infections eat away at it - lovely), and I was probably eight years old at the time. I recall being completely enthralled while watching Morecambe and Wise on television.

I said, without taking my eyes from the TV, in a serious tone and with a grim face, 'Oh, it's just amusing.' What I recall - and what would explain my tone - is that I was enthralled by the idea that I was watching two grown-ups being ridiculous. It was such a relief to watch adults play, muck around, and laugh. It wasn't something to giggle about; it was a serious issue! If there were ways to be ridiculous and get laughs on this thing called television, I wanted to be a part of it, because I couldn't stand to live in a world where I couldn't perform, dance, sing, and act foolishly. That didn't seem like a life worth living.

This is a somewhat sad reflection on two events that all too frequently occur in life. To begin, youngsters are frequently instructed, 'Shush, don't be stupid.' Not that I blame any parent in the land for saying that statement. Of course, when a youngster is being noisy, showing off, or repeating themselves over and over, any good parent will eventually lose patience and yell, 'Just stop being ridiculous.'

I recall when a family member said that to me, and it was a watershed moment. One that I am now grateful for. I could not comprehend why someone would wish to limit my genuine happiness. So when I saw Eric Morecambe grinning at me via a television camera, I fell in love with him and humor.

The second reason my little self was knocked over by these two mature guys clowning for my delight was that witnessing grownups playing was evidently uncommon.

It's amazing and emotional to discover from a 'ist' that your guess from your little life experience was true. I was even more surprised that my judgment was correct when he remarked that 'for extremely competitive, serious people, to realize later in life that they had missed this thrill can be terrible'.

My point is that we recognize that the so-called wonderful and energetic early years were all about developing aspects of ourselves in employment, finances, finding a family, and so on, in order to feel safe or to be in continual service, all at the expense of joy.

Stuart Brown stated that this arises because of the 'culturally accepted perception that people who play are shallow, are not living in the real world, are dilettantes or amoral slackers'. If we are admonished at a young age not to be stupid, we will naturally fear being playful in our thirties, forties, and fifties. It's why people enjoy getting older. It's when you hear, 'Oh, I've just stopped worrying what other people say,' that you know they're free to play again. It is very kind to give ourselves delight.

My experience of losing joy was ironic. The memory of seeing Morecambe and Wise as a child on the floor of my parents' sitting room returned thirty years later, when I was sitting on the floor of my own sitting room, surrounded by a swarm of index cards with narrative ideas for my own comedy show. I was not a playful adult who joyfully pursued their childhood goal; I was a stressed adult who felt the burden of the job.

My personal sense of play had gradually degraded over the previous two decades. And I did had a nagging feeling that something was missing. Badly. And free. I wanted to join a choir. I hadn't played tennis in years, despite it being one of my favorite activities. I didn't spend enough time in nature. The small and large things that provided me joy have gradually faded from my life. It is not a favorable situation if any of our professions, duties, or problems cause us to prioritize everything except recreation. However, I had not previously learned that play was crucial to my health. I was aware that my life had lost some equilibrium, but I had no idea how serious the consequences were.

But, like me putting dancing lessons on my list every year for over a decade, if we don't do them again, there's no need to beat ourselves up: we're doing our best, and there's probably a deeper reason why. That is why I will continue to urge, "Let's find those patterns we're in and smash them so we can be freer, healthier, and have the energy and meaning we want but may have lost."

Personally, I refuse to have the world tell me that I don't have time for joy or that if I do, I should 'stop being stupid'. I feel the world should be disappointed and shocked to see how little time we now have for play. Even my eight-year-old self, who watched comedy, realized this. This, to me, is more evidence that the wild self, which is fundamental in all of us, always knows how things should be.

# Serious Business

In my twenties, I worked as an office manager and PA in the nonprofit sector, and I had the best bosses. There was one humorous incident when our boss arrived into the stationery cupboard and found three of his administrative staff sitting in chairs with damp hair, waiting for the fourth friend to cut our hair. He assumed we were doing some obligatory office supply inventory. In fact, we had created a temporary salon. It was a little break, but we'd make up the time.

He knew we'd be back to our desks with smiles on our faces (and fresh haircuts), ready to work with new energy. We like what we did, we appreciated what the organization stood for (it had a why), and we could get down to business without complaint. But we needed to get out and play. We were a group of twenty-somethings who were not yet burdened with responsibility or worried about being labeled as unserious or lazy. Probably because we were not defined by our occupations.

One element that contributed to my loss of delight was that I began to take my work seriously, considering it as a career. Jobs will be stressful and time-consuming. That cannot be prevented. However, with a 'why' and a balance of joy, pressures can be accepted as part of the profession rather than depleting it.

We may have a work that we want to master and should invest in, yet pressure increases as we lose delight. What a terrible example to set for our children, don't you think, MDRC? We are instilling in them the belief that adulthood is all about doing, that it is necessary to become very 'serious' and 'important'.

I'll tell you what's extremely serious about job - not playing.

Not simply the essential health benefits. The things I'll remember about my colleagues aren't the sequences we did or their mastery of their craft, as impressive as it was, but the behind-the-scenes drama. They are just being themselves.

And if it was a playful moment, that will be the first and most treasured memory. Although the time I arrived into a rehearsal wearing three well-placed promotional stickers for the play we were rehearsing may be one my colleagues want to forget... Moving on...

## Don't Be Childish'

I was amused to see that, in the spirit of letting masks fall with The Boy from Bristol (MDRC, I couldn't deny the frisson any longer and didn't hesitate to continue to rendezvous with him), the guard of silliness was one of the most difficult. I probably showed him the Lego and cooked a cake half-naked because I needed confirmation regarding my concern of being overly dramatic or immature. That can only be a culturally conditioned phobia.

What was I supposed to do, don a bonnet and recite something on the pianoforte? When I was as ridiculous as I naturally wanted to be, I had the most fun. When we laughed the most. When we felt the most connected. A mask cannot be worn while playing because it is so wild. If it does, it is not playable.

It seems odd to tell older children and young adults, 'Don't be childish' (following on from 'Don't be silly'). I once asked my niece what her favorite time of day was. She mentioned the evening, and I responded, 'Oh yes, me too, because it's bedtime and we can start relaxing.' She looked perplexed and responded, 'No, because I'm so thrilled for the next day.' I had to acknowledge, with a heavy heart, that at the moment, I was battling with a lack of energy and was rarely looking forward to the next day. That hit hard; we can never experience the same day twice. Every day is precious.

Shouldn't we be humble enough to learn, or relearn, from the young? They should turn around and say, 'We're not being childish. We're playing because it's the nicest part of the day and really excellent for us; please join in.

# Pacing and Presence

## Intentional Pottering

One of my favorite pleasures is pottering. I don't mean walking; in fact, a potter's stride is nothing like that of a walker. There is no haste, only a calm, intentional, and soothing amble. Consider this the shuffling of an Italian nonagenarian.

Needless to say, twenty-two-year-olds may not understand what I mean by 'deliberate pottering'. Please don't think I'm referring to purposeful pottery. I believe all potters are quite intentional; otherwise, there'd be carnage with clay flying left, right, and center in any given pottery class - "Marjorie, can you be more intentional, please? The handle of your jug hit me in the face.' Though I admit I did create small carnage in my pottery class, my head is filled with hilarious images. The other potters gasped as the pots wobbled, and then they all looked at me. I chose to wave enthusiastically with a jaunty, public school, 'Hello, potting peeps!' I was also unable to resist building artificial noses for myself and a pal to play with.

Let's get back to my pottery hobby. My favorite thing about it is how completely and delightfully mild it feels. To move gradually at the opposite pace of the hectic world, allowing time to breathe and absorb everything around you. Time to gaze up. In fact, my watchword for this resource is gentleness. Ah, the joy of tenderness.

We live in a world that seems to lack gentleness. However, inside our abrasive, concrete institutions, there will be breathtaking moments of softness that we rarely witness. A instructor whispers words of encouragement. A nurse extends her hand and takes a time to smile and breathe with a patient. Perhaps if we can cultivate more moments of gentleness in this hectic society, we can help slow it - and ourselves - down to a more natural pace. A slow revolution toward tenderness.

It may appear pointless and ridiculous to suggest that some intentional pottering is a good place to start, but it has been the most effective of my slowing down trials. There's even a scientific reason to potter, MDRC. If we haste, we send signals to our brain that we may be in danger; the neurological system reacts and fires up in anticipation, creating a rise in cortisol and adrenaline. It was also interesting to note how shallow my breathing became when I was rushing. Shallow breathing also signals to our brain that we are under peril. Slowing down relaxes our bodies because the brain perceives, 'Oh, we are moving more slowly, right, we are safe now, stand down.' It was another element to decreasing my chronic stress reaction. Things continued to feel lighter.

There are still just twenty-four hours in a day, but when I go slower, it feels like I've created more time. Life becomes simpler and softer. Slowing down also allows me to be more intentional about the activities and chores I choose to complete during the day, as well as how I go about them and how long I spend on them.

I was encouraged yet again by how the riches revealed themselves to be gentle. They frequently felt compelled to pursue another goal. But not the valuables. Despite their depth of insight, they were only pleasant offerings.

If merely slowing down is a simple prescription to help our brain and body perform effectively, I strongly advise you to try pottering - slow your walking pace from A to B, complete everyday home duties more slowly, and pause and take three deep breaths before checking your email. Everything makes a difference.


A excellent technique for women, especially those with larger breasts, is to practice deliberate pottering while not wearing a bra! I feel carefree the moment I remove my bra. I may feel the weight of the breast, but the weight of life is gone! You are quite welcome, MDRC, for the visions I have just imagined for you; it is my joy.

# How You Do One Thing Is How You Do Everything

I'm not sure who coined the term 'How you do one thing is how you do everything', but I believe it's wonderful. It demonstrated to me that the problem is with how we do things rather than what we do.

It reminded me of when I was thinking about incorporating the emergency walk into my comedy and found myself doing it in a shopping mall. The emergency stroll began as I mumbled, 'Fine, I'll just march across the dumb mall and find the stupid business myself if the stupid map is that stupidly incomprehensible.' I heard a wise whisper: Miranda, how you do one thing is how you do everything. Did I want to be an unpleasant, angry marcher in all I do? No, I wished to be a tranquil lady who glided gracefully through life gently, playfully, peacefully, and forcefully.

If I could practice this at a shopping mall, I'd be more likely to be this person on days when I needed to be at my best. I began to walk in a 'elegant waft' style. And there it was: as soon as I slowed my speed, I had time to appreciate what was around me, I smiled at someone, and I felt instantaneously nicer! The task would still be completed, but now with values and health intact.

It's not what you do that matters, but how you feel while doing it. In that time, I also improved my own self-care. MDRC, that is what it keeps coming back to. When we really feel that our intrinsic individuality is valuable, we cease seeing ourselves as something to be fixed. Instead, we honor the way we work best. We then feel safe to move at our own pace, allowing us to be present for all the good that would otherwise be missed if we ran.

Don't flee from yourself, MDRC; you are a magnificent elephant!

# Don't Fear the Setback

## Help, I'm Going Backwards

It wasn't until I had a chronic disease that I realized I was afraid of taking a step backwards. I discovered that I could not calmly and maturely accept any health setbacks.

Anything resembling a setback in my physical rehabilitation would send me into a tantrum, spewing petulant sentiments like, Why does this always happen to me?, It's not fair, or Everyone else has a lot easier time of it.

I believe that part of my inability to deal with setbacks stemmed from my lack of experience with failure. Let me quickly address that, MDRC - I am not familiar with the dread of failure. I've experienced some epic fails. Certainly in my professional life. I just didn't see them as such. In general, I laughed them off. I'll tell you a story about an audition that most of my acting pals would be horrified by.

It was early in my professional acting career, and I was ecstatic to earn a role in a comedic drama starring Martin Clunes. I completed the scenes, thought I did well, and had a wonderful and unique experience.

A few months later, my agent called to say that they were going to write her role for the next season, where she would be a regular character. Right now, this was quite exciting. 'This is it!' I explained to my agency. 'This may be a big break.' She was equally thrilled for me. She informed me that I would be meeting with the producers to discuss the part. Of course, having previously played the character, I reasoned that they would be interested in some of my suggestions.

I attended the meeting and was instructed to wait in the hallway outside the office. The producer's assistant then handed me several sheets of screenplays. I thanked her and felt pleased, smiling confidently at the other people in the hallway. They all seemed worried, and I assumed there was an audition going on in another room because they were all studying and murmuring over their scripts.

I strolled confidently into my meeting, completed the reading, discussed the part, and was pleased with how it went. The next day, I called my agent to see what the next steps would be. She had to break the news to me that I was not the only one auditioning for the part that day. I maintained a long silence.

I find that amusing because a 'failed' audition does not bother me. It doesn't undermine my confidence or self-esteem.

Setbacks are inevitable in everyone's lives, but they only cause tension, tantrums, and deep disappointment when they are linked to our most unpleasant experiences and fear-inducing limiting beliefs. I know a friend who considered any relationship ending as a sign that she was better off alone, and she assumed that people judged her as impossible to be with and that everything was her fault. I was afraid I wouldn't get well.

I know that many others who have had similar illnesses, particularly energy-sapping ones like extended Covid and ME, as well as those who have endured the agony of waiting for news of remission from any illness, will be aware of the anxiety of a setback. In energy-related settings, these setbacks are sometimes referred to as a crash, dip, or flare-up. Simply put, it is a time when your body feels as if it has failed you and you are 'back there'. The dread of regressing, having symptoms return, or having to go through something again is understandable.

Fear not, MDRC; there were pearls to be discovered as I delved into this trove. I have your back on the backwards steps.

## Stop Comparing

Now this was something I excelled at! Constantly comparing. Comparison is something that might exacerbate or even create a setback. Getting stuck in comparison can be triggered by 'I should be further along' thinking, which leads to us making incorrect judgments about where we are - or are not - in life. All of this is a big gigantic lie!

It would be difficult to discuss comparisons without considering social media. It's too big a deal to go into detail here, but let's just say I wasn't very nice to myself during the Silly Setback of Doom, Drudge, and Despair because I looked through Instagram. I thought I knew better and had overcome that tendency. My fate threw all of my personal policies out the window! It resulted in a severe episode of comparison.

I came across photos of pals in Capri, on a rooftop bar with a pool in London, by a river in Surrey, in a beautiful pub garden, and in their own garden with family eating ice lollipops. Seeing all of this made me feel more trapped by my restrictions. I'll own it, I was jealous.

Fortunately, before I could criticize myself for feeling envious, I discovered that it is not only normal, but it also explains why we may be restless and dissatisfied. While it is unpleasant to experience, it is a powerful emotional warning signal that reminds us of our ideals. With freedom as one of my top ideals and adventure and nature as two of my big joys, all of those images hit me hard.

Comparison and envy also remind us that we are essentially judging others, believing they are having the best time possible. Comparing our so-called tiny lives to their apparent large ones. It's so simple to believe that the grass is greener. This is not a loving position since we do not see any vulnerability or need for support. Brené Brown's quote: "If we pay attention, most people have a story that will bring us to our knees." resonates with me. How readily we lose that when we are caught up in comparison.

The best phrase I know about comparison that helps me be nice is: you can't compare your insides to someone else's outsides. It is far kinder to ourselves and others to stay in our own lane, because there is only one of us, and how we run our own race of life is unique to each of us. Do not arrive at the finish line disorganized and weary. Fly past that line knowing you've raced in your own lane, not against anyone else.

Trying to get into someone else's lane will always lead to trouble. Broken record alert. MDRC, there has only been one of you in all of human history. You should never compare yourself to another! Speaking of records, I'm going to take another song break. Pat Benatar's 'We Belong' is a must-listen for any 80s child.

# Keep Going, My Love, Keep Going!

Following my major health setback, my body gradually restored to a more energetic and functional state as I submitted more and more. Little Patti and I were getting into a wonderful rhythm, and my morning routine now included 'playing parrot'. Before you jump to any unsettling conclusions, that simply means throwing Patti's toy parrot for her to fetch; it was a welcome dose of play to begin the day. Things were going really well until - and I almost dare not say this, MDRC, but I hope you've come to realize that we don't need to be afraid of setbacks - there was another 'setback'! Life is undoubtedly a roller coaster.

My sentiments for The Boy from Bristol grew stronger as I spent more time with him. And then. We needed to take a break. I know-- ouch. There were several reasons why we weren't sure if the time was right to become a 'us'. It was hard. It hurt my heart. A lot. I wasn't sure if it was the end, or if circumstances would finally allow us to continue getting to know each other. It was difficult since the connection, safety, kindness, laughter, and tenderness that had so greatly aided my recuperation were suddenly absent.

The disconnection left a brief awful vacuum. A flashback to earlier loneliness, and the need I had dared to feel not to be alone. I didn't get trapped because I had the tools to let those feelings to exist and flow through me. Thank you, Treasure Three. Finally, I trusted that, like whether or not I would receive an audition, everything would work out in the end, and that I was capable of dealing with whatever course it took. When there is a foundation of trust, it makes an enormous impact in how people live their lives.

I was also thankful because I knew, deep down in my core, that even if I didn't get those traits from The Boy, they were the most important things in life to focus on. I was going to accept responsibility for adhering to the ideals I knew I needed, which were healing my body of weariness and viruses. We can't delegate responsibility for ourselves any more than we can assume accountability for others.

I was also able to demonstrate my patience in the face of any setbacks caused by a painful heart. Perseverance was a difficult trait to acquire, but I had succeeded. And I had the other Patience: Patti the puppy.

It might be Patti and me, following Peggy and me... My next dog husband...!

# It's All About Love in the End

## Hang On A Minute ...

I expected my treasure hunt to stop at Treasure Nine! I expected to emerge from the cave blinking like a fifty-year-old heavy foal eager to begin life again. But before I could take my first step into new land, I was struck by another huge revvy. I summoned my newfound patience and sat symbolically in the cave's entryway (physically in my armchair, overlooking my garden). I took a deep breath, quieted my mind, and focused on what this final epiphany was attempting to tell me.

It turned out to be quite the treasure, well worth our time. And it is one that I shall express as clearly as possible in our final chapter together. Here we go...

I came to the conclusion that if, as I discovered when overcoming setbacks in Treasure Nine, the solution to my basic concerns and issues was knowing that I could seek for help and meet my needs, then our most primal fear must ultimately be that of being alone. Feeling alone makes it difficult to meet our basic necessities. We can't ask for help, cry with others, show our vulnerability, rest, or find joy easily. The list of prior treasure's healing components continues indefinitely.

The treasures, more than anything else, appeared to alleviate feelings of isolation and detachment. To ourselves and one another. This brings us full circle back to our core identity—the need to belong. And, I believe, MDRC, what that actually means is LOVE.

I had hints that, whatever else I learned along the way, love would be the answer. If love - both receiving and expressing love - is our ultimate identity, isn't life about learning to love? I believe I can really say that my knowledge of what it meant to start over - after everything I had gone through - is entirely about understanding myself, honoring that self, and treating myself with kindness and respect. As a result, I discover that I have the ability and want to love outwardly, consciously.

Humans are neurobiologically predisposed to both receiving and giving love. Everything else is noise.

When we remove the noise. When we remove worldly non-serving aspirations. When we take away everything we crave. When we take away the success that we work so hard for. When we take away all of the takeout we want to eat (I meant 'take away food').

There's a reason why the most common regret of the dying is this one. There's a reason we often say 'just be yourself' to our loved ones: we recognize who they are, their strengths, and wonders before they do. Setting yourself and others free with love is what gives my life significance. Our best legacy. We carry forth our human design.

We may have loved by giving advice, smiling at a stranger, donating money, offering employment, working hard for something or someone we believed in, parenting, caring for or rescuing an animal, encouraging someone, listening, reminding someone to care for themselves and the environment, or creating a piece of work or a garden. There are numerous ways we can express love.

It is quite difficult to express the emotion of love. And who am I to attempt, when some of our best poets haven't always succeeded? Instead, I'll make a practical proposal for individuals who may have had to acquire or relearn the concept after painful experiences that eroded their conviction in it. For me, it began in my head: to believe that I was loved and lovable simply by existing. My faith has helped me. Then, in order to cement that truth in my heart, I had to make an effort to seek out this inexplicable, illusive energy and power at work among us.

I had been overly focused on the invisible bodily symptoms I was experiencing. So I started small. I would notice a hospital receptionist's warm gaze and smile as she assured me that everything would be fine, and I would consciously allow myself to feel loved by it. Even if the sun shone on a special day for me, or if I sat down with a great hot cocoa on a cold winter day, I would reinterpret everything as love. Let alone when someone assisted me, gave me a present, or complimented me. By observing all of the different types of love around me every day, I began to rewire away from any negative thoughts that had crept in, telling me that I was alone in my issues or that life was simply too difficult.

If my attempt to represent love in a practical way fails to strike a chord, let me to sow some love science. I believe we have the capacity to do further academic research, MDRC...

It becomes far beyond my pay grade to explore much deeper, but I just about comprehended this next interesting section because of what I had learned in prior treasures: human biological evolution demonstrates that our fetal brain leaves us completely dependant on others. It is critical that we have nurturing, loving influences around us because our brains double in size throughout our first year. As a result, our psychological and social development is heavily influenced by our early years. However, the 'ists' indicate that we may adapt and overcome the bad impacts of childhood through our friend neuroplasticity. Things can change for all of us, MDRC, regardless of our starting point in life.

According to science, when we love ourselves and one another, our health improves. Feeling loved makes us feel safe, and feeling safe allows our nervous system to function normally. As we now know, our nervous system is crucial because it interacts with our other critical systems (immune, cardiovascular, endocrine, muscular, lymphatic, and respiratory) to allow our organs to work properly.

There you have it. Love is more than simply a lovely idea. It maintains the mind, brain, and body healthy. Again, wow.

I've heard many individuals remark, 'I just want my kids to be happy.' It's natural to prioritize the happiness of our loved ones. (Of course, we want it.) What if they are unable to be happy for some reason? What if they lose their health? What happens if their marriage fails or they lose a partner? What happens if their dream job never materializes? What if they reside in a country where war has broken out? We may not understand the misery and evil that still exists in this world, but we are aware of it.

I wonder if wanting ourselves and our loved ones to be happy is a stressful endeavor. Happiness might be lost at any time. If that's taken away, we'll need some cake. If you truly want someone to be happy, you should never make them feel uneasy or unconfident about who they are; you should let them know they are nice and cherished. And you'll know they're going to be healthy and live their lives to the fullest, loving others regardless of the circumstances.

That is it.

Is anything else really important?

Sitting in the entryway at the end of this nearly decade-long cave, I can take another look at the treasures. Suddenly, it becomes evident that each one serves as a guide for better loving ourselves and others. None of them fall outside that scope. Each treasure is kind. Upbuilding and encouraging. Each one contributes to our understanding of how to feel and offer love. Each one smashes a pattern of insignificant noise. Coincidence? When is it proven that humans are wired to love and be loved? Not for me!

My small niece once said, while listening to her grandparents recount the history of warring countries, 'Why doesn't everyone simply get along? I do not comprehend it. Well, quite and indeed! Whenever I've had debates about faith, they've always concluded with the basic accord - mystery of faith aside - that if everyone did unto others as they would have done unto them, the world would be a better place. Again, quite, and indeed!

As we love ourselves more, we love others more, and as we love others more, we love ourselves more, resulting in an ever-increasing cycle of individual and universal wellness.

That was really worth sitting down for. Thank you, Cave. You came from a place of misery, and you were unpleasant to begin with, but you taught me everything I needed to become better and start over. I am now less opposed to the adage, 'The only way out is through'!

I hope I could end it there. But then... Love is not easy.

We live in a society - one I find excruciating to acknowledge - in which love may be twisted, controlled, and perverted, robbing people of their faith in the very thing they require the most. And so, MDRC, I'd want to share with you some last patterns that, when broken, can help us return to a state of love.

# Chapter 4: WILD AND HOME

## The Final Goodbye

The countless moments, analogies, experiences, and stories of the last decade have resulted in one important realization: I have finally returned to my wild self. It is a certain emotion, but I'm not sure how to convey it. Part of me wants to avoid even attempting it. If my final thoughts are scatty or unwittingly poetic(!), I hope some truths inside them land or make sense. For we've gone this far together, My Dearest Reader Chum, and I'd be remiss not to finish the story with you. Because, after all, this is our final goodbye. Plus, there's one detail I'm eager to tell you.

I used to despise goodbyes, but now I see them as an opportunity to praise the person, time, or experience; I'm more grateful if something is difficult to say goodbye to, because it indicates it was much more valuable. Mostly, the pain of saying goodbye has subsided since I can now look ahead with confidence rather than anxiety. With an inner quietness that gives me strength. That is undoubtedly a new beginning, and I am not sad to say goodbye to any of the previous effort and worry. Oh, have I gone 'poetic' already?!

I've mostly said my goodbyes to Lyme disease-induced ME. I will always have my past with me, but it no longer defines who I am. When it does lead me, such as having to manage weariness, I rarely fear it (it is simply boring and tries my patience!). Mainly because I now understand the mind-body link and am hopeful for a complete recovery. My ordeal is gone now that I have the discipline to keep working on the tools that lessen the stress reaction and the surrender to let go of what I cannot control.

As I continue to slow down, rest, notice what habits I need to break and what intentions I need to cultivate, detach from judgement and criticism, manage my energy, celebrate regularly, stay grateful and playful, and follow a pressure-free purpose to love (accepting that I will fail in some way every day), I am letting go of patterns that have never served me well. The old techniques that produce harmful stress are withering and shriveling up (physically and neuroscientifically, good!).

Every day, I may have to say goodbye to an old habit that has yet to be undone or an old reaction that has yet to be entirely rewired, but I also know that there is hope for regeneration.

I have new norms to greet.

# It's All Grace

I knew I was going to start over, from a different perspective, and that the second half of my life would be vastly different. At the same time, I didn't want to undo everything that had happened previously.

I jotted down a list of instances from my unimportant yet significant existence; when it dawned on me that I had no control over almost anything, I smiled. How arrogant of us to believe we have complete control over the majority of our life. How stupid that we strive to control things we can't and become upset when they don't go our way. I sighed a big sigh of relief; I don't have much control. What bliss is this?!

Everything truly excellent in my life had come from grace. The list was very long - I wrote everything down, from a dying woman sending me her book Call the Midwife and saying it was being made for TV and she hoped I'd play Chummy, to the fact that I have no control over the creative ideas that come to me or what I am naturally good at.

I'll spare you the list of my life (though I encourage it) and instead offer you the one I've been itching to share:

I had no control over the fact that I met my closest friend and the love of my life, who offers me more silliness, laughing, joy, support, care, and safety than I ever imagined possible in a person, because I lost my house due to mold illness and he was the building surveyor on the remediation project.

Yes, MDRC, I loved Mr Mould Man! The one and the same.

I'm not saying you need a moldy house or anything like that to find redemption in your life, but I do believe that suffering can lead to good.

May my Mr Mould Man / The Boy / The Boy from Bristol / The Boyfriend not just be a rom-com story, but also our constant hope, MDRC. When I told any of my pals that I had met someone, they all just paused, perplexed, and said, 'HOW?!' With housebound disease and a global pandemic, it's unlikely that a knight in shining armour will materialize on your doorstep. But he did. To de-mold me

# Acknowledgements

I often read acknowledgements in books, but I am not sure why! Perhaps I read them in books I actually adored, savouring every last word. Sometimes a book becomes such a friend that I don't want it to end, and the acknowledgements are the last traces of my connection with the author.

That motivates me to acknowledge the brave, bright, and beautiful women who have inspired and taught me so much. The list might be much longer, but Brené Brown, Caroline Leaf, Sue Monk Kidd, Martha Beck, Edith Eger, and Byron Katie have all been extremely helpful to me in recent years, and I am grateful for their efforts. They are very much a part of the treasure. I want to be their best buddy.

Julia Voce, a genius storyteller, is already a closest friend and has introduced me to other greats such as Elizabeth Gilbert, Tara Brach, Ellen Langer, Maya Angelou, and Mary Oliver. Thank you, Jools, for your friendship during the difficult times, for loving Peggy and Patti (!) and for valiantly reading an early manuscript of the book while shouting 'don't understand' or 'bored now'. This book required skilled candour and wisdom! That's genuine friendship.

I'd like to thank my sister and a group of friends for surprising me on my 50th birthday with a list of words they thought best described me. It was a risk, and I believe one person used the word 'windy', but it was one of the most precious gifts I have ever received: spreading the seed of how we are defined beyond worldly standards, as well as encouragement that my story and what I had learned were worth communicating. Forever grateful.

Thank you to Jo Rice, Jess Thompson, Pete Grieg, Alice Goodwin-Hudson, Sydney Jenkins, Rose Heiney, Simon Sinek, and Christine Dunkley for reading the book before it was published. Your remarks were extremely useful and encouraging. And thank you to Mo Vernon, who transcribed all of my interminable research notes years ago. Mo, you helped me get started on the lengthy process.

And Emma Abrahams (keep an eye out for her name as an actor) - you helped me finish it by providing actual and figurative neighborly care and love, as well as efficient administrative aid. (And don't forget that you created the best-selling 'I bloody love crisps' bowl and pen at The Miranda Shop - clever!)

There have been many outstanding doctors and practitioners who did not 'tatt' on me. I won't use your entire names here because you might feel overwhelmed, but thank you Debbie, Laura, Michael, Louise, Peg, Amelia, Jennifer, Jess, Sarah, Ed, Alan, and John.

Finally, without these two men, this book would not exist. The Boy, or rather The Husband, who listened with patience and care not only to sections of the book, but also to the frustrations of the process and the fear of not finishing it. And fed me numerous lunches and snacks along the route to keep me going. Husband, you are certainly the best present in my life (not just the meals and snacks). You brought my joy back.

And then there's my agent, Gordon Wise of Curtis Brown. He has been one of the most loyal, patient, and compassionate persons in my professional life, supporting me through all of the painful ups and downs of illness and refusing to let go until I had a diagnosis and the chance of returning to work. Thanks, Gordon.

And thank you for sending publishing queen Louise Moore my not-always-great poems to see what she thought. Thank you, Louise, for not understanding anything about poetry, whether it was good or horrible (your words), and for daring to meet with me to discuss whether I could share my tale! And thank you, Louise, for connecting me to editor extraordinaire Jill Taylor, who made my ramblings and research make sense.

And thank you for laughing with me along the road and supporting me by sharing how the treasures benefitted you (as well as advice on shoes and clothing!) Thank you very much, Louise and Jill, and your Penguin team, for making it possible for me to return to work for the first time in a long time, allowing me to work while recovering. I am sincerely appreciative.

This process has taught me more than any other that we need to connect and support one another in order to be the best versions of ourselves. I'll never 'go it alone' again.

The contents of this book may not be copied, reproduced or transmitted without the express written permission of the author or publisher. Under no circumstances will the publisher or author be responsible or liable for any damages, compensation or monetary loss arising from the information contained in this book, whether directly or indirectly. .

Disclaimer Notice:

Although the author and publisher have made every effort to ensure the accuracy and completeness of the content, they do not, however, make any representations or warranties as to the accuracy, completeness, or reliability of the content. , suitability or availability of the information, products, services or related graphics contained in the book for any purpose. Readers are solely responsible for their use of the information contained in this book

Every effort has been made to make this book possible. If any omission or error has occurred unintentionally, the author and publisher will be happy to acknowledge it in upcoming versions.

Copyright © 2024

All rights reserved.

Printed in Dunstable, United Kingdom